Classic Hotels ... on a par with the best Championship Courses.

A brace of fine hotels set within the magnificent Highlands specializing in the best Golfing Holidays available. Famous championship courses on your doorstep, with another seventeen within easy reach. Catering for players of all standards, from the budding amateur to the true professional.

Both hotels offer excellent two centre breaks, adept golf itinerary assistance and tee booking service.

NAIRN
Seabank Road Nairn
By Inverness Scotland
IV12 4HD

DORNOCH
The 1st Tee Dornoch
Sutherland Scotland
IV25 3LG

For brochure, reservations or advice contact Susan on 0667 52301 Fax: 0667 55267 for either hotel.

We pride ourselves on customer service . . . so good you'll want to come back.

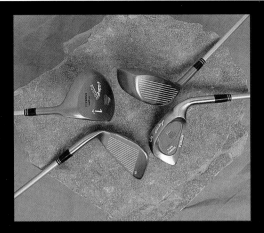

Vantage Fusion

The Vantage Fusion model is proof that high quality golf clubs do not necessarily have to be expensive.

Fusion irons are a very modern peripheral over-size design which is forgiving to the golfer who is looking to improve their game.

Fusion metalwoods have a slightly larger clubhead which combined with its conventional shape produces a solid feel and enables extra control.

The Fusion is available with Rapport Graphite shafts or with True Temper steel shafts.

VANTAGE GOLF,
Unit 2 Manfield Park,
Guildford Road,
Cranleigh, Surrey
GU6 8PT.
Tel: 0483 278281
Fax: 0483 27827

BRITISH GOLF MUSEUM
St. Andrews, Scotland

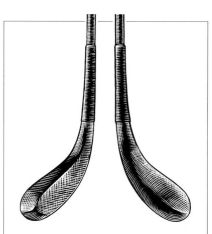

Since it opened in 1990, the British Golf Museum has received international recognition for its innovative display techniques which bring the history of golf alive. The museum has received seven awards from various bodies within the fields of tourism, audio-visual technology and architecture. Situated opposite the Royal and Ancient Golf Club it is administered by the Royal and Ancient Golf Club Trust and is open to the public seven days in the summer and five days in the winter.

Four key ingredients for a successful museum are all brought together in the British Golf Museum . These are the need to tell a strong story, the need to be visually striking, and the need to entertain as well as educate. Each gallery has a well-defined theme; each display case within the gallery tells a story related to that theme and each object on display contributes to that story.

The museum is set out chronologically, taking the visitor through the earliest surviving written reference to golf in 1475 right up to golf clubs and articles donated by modern-day heroes such as Arnold Palmer, Jack Nicklaus and Nick Faldo.

Philips Compact Disc Interactive systems are an important feature of the museum. There are twelve monitors all detailing the many aspects of golf and the administration of the Royal and Ancient Golf Club; a quiz on the rules of golf and indepth history of players ancient and modern. The latest and most fascinating disc offers an interesting journey through time, tracing the origins of the game 500 years ago and relives its memorable moments up to 1945. Included is an exciting match play, ghostly play-off game on the Old Course in St. Andrews and a fascinating trivia game. To round it all off, the museum has an Audio-Visual theatre, a shop and a car park.

TAKE THE FAMILY FOR A WALK ROUND THE WOODS.

 There are five hundred years of golfing history, and a great day out waiting to be discovered at the British Golf Museum. Enjoy the journey, as the latest Philips CD-i and touch-screen displays guide you through the game's history with stories of famous golfers and tournaments.

See the royal, the ancient, and the modern champion's golf clubs, clothing and memorabilia. Discover why a King banned the game. Learn the difference between a mashie and a spoon. Then finish the round at our gift shop.

The British Golf Museum,
Bruce Embankment, St Andrews, Fife KY16 9AB.
Telephone: 0334 78880.

CONTENTS

Cover Design by Jennifer Thomson, Edinburgh

Pastime Publications Ltd gratefully acknowledge the assistance of The Scottish Tourist Board, Area Tourist Boards, The Royal and Ancient Golf Club of St. Andrews and the United States Golf Association, Donald Ford, Dougie Donnelly, John Chillas and others in compiling this guide.

First published by The Scottish Tourist Board 1970.
U.K. Distribution by A.A. Publishing Ltd.
Typesetting by Newtext Composition Ltd.
Printed and Bound by Eyre & Spottiswoode Ltd.
Worldwide distribution by The British Tourist Authority.

ADVERTISERS' INDEX

SEE ALSO COLOUR ADVERTS

⋏

RULES OF GOLF

Principal Changes introduced in the 1992 Code

DEFINITIONS
The terms "line of putt" and "line of play" are defined.

RULES
Rule 4–1e. Club Face
The restriction with regard to insets or attachments on metal clubs is eliminated.

Rule 4–4a. Selection and Replacement of Clubs
The addition or replacement of a club or clubs may not be made by borrowing any club selected for play by any other person playing on the course.

Rule 5–3 Ball Unfit for Play)
Rule 12–2. Identifying Ball)
If the player fails to carry out a part or parts of the procedure he is penalised only one stroke.

Rule 13–4. Ball Lying in or Touching Hazard
Expanded to state that if a ball lies in a hazard there is no penalty (provided nothing is done which constitutes testing the condition of the hazard or improves the lie of the ball) if the player touches the ground or water in a water hazard as a result of or to prevent falling, in removing an obstruction, in measuring or in retrieving or lifting a ball under any Rule.

Rule 24–2c. Ball Lost
There is an addition to the Rule to make provision for a ball lost in an immovable obstruction.

APPENDIX II
4–1a. General
Limited adjustability is permitted in the design of putters.

4–1c. Grip
If a putter has two grips, both of the grips must be circular in cross-section. However, putters which do not conform with this Rule may continue to be used until 31st December 1992.

The Spalding Top-Flite XL^{II}

The Spalding Top-Flite XLII

The world's best selling golf ball now goes a bit further.

A B E R D E E N S H I R E

A N G U S

HOTEL

A superb mansion house hotel, totally re-furbished, overlooking sea front with superb en-suite accommodation and two first class restaurants. With several superb golf courses on our door step, including the famous Carnoustie Championship Course, let us organise your golfing break.

For further information please contact:

**General Manager,
Windmill Hotel,
Millgate Loan,
Arbroath DD11 1QG.
Tel: (0241) 72278.
Fax: (0241) 430441.**

STB   AA ★★

$CHAPELBANK$ House HOTEL and RESTAURANT

Elegant town house with four luxurious bedrooms. This family run hotel offers first class cuisine. Ideally situated for golf, fishing, shooting, hillwalking and visiting the Glens and castles of Angus.

**S.T.B.
4 Crowns Highly Commended.
69 East High Street,Forfar DD8 2EP.Tel: (0307) 63151.**

A
N
G
U
S

LETHAM GRANGE HOTEL & GOLF COURSES

In the heartland of golf lies the superb Letham Grange Hotel and Golf Courses. The magnificent Victorian Mansion nestles within the panoramic Letham Grange Estate. The Mansion has been restored to its former glory as a top quality, 3 star hotel with 20 bedrooms, offering a style which is both traditional and sumptuous.

36 holes of magnificent golf! Widely acclaimed as one of the premier courses in Scotland, the Old Course provides a blend of tree lined parkland and open rolling fairways. With water playing a major role, the course is both scenic and dramatic. The New Course, although slightly shorter - and without the water hazards, offers golfers a more relaxed and less arduous round. However, it can be deceptive!

For further information on special golfing breaks or a day's golf please contact:

**Letham Grange Hotel, Colliston, by Arbroath DD11 4RL
Tel: (0241) 890373. Fax: (0241) 890414.**   COMMENDED ▼▼▼▼

station hotel
STATION ROAD, CARNOUSTIE

Under personal family supervision, the Station Hotel offers first class holiday accommodation. Situated near to the world famous golf courses, setting for many Open Golf Championships. The hotel specialises in weekend and golfing breaks. Traditional Scottish meals are temptingly served with ample portions by our friendly and efficient staff.

CONTACT: MR. IVOR FARMER (0241) 52447

FOR ROAD MAPS SEE PAGES 133-138

**A
Y
R
S
H
I
R
E**

PLEASE TURN TO PAGE 93 FOR LISTS OF GOLF COURSES

A
Y
R
S
H
I
R
E

24

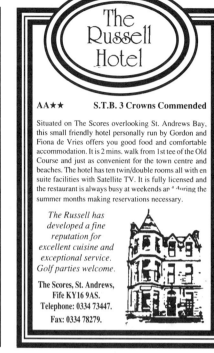

TO ASSIST WITH HOLIDAY ENQUIRIES SEE OUR BOOKING FORMS ON PAGES 139-143

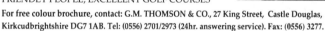

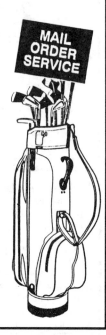

L O T H I A N

The Original

Old Clubhouse

at Gullane

Lounge Bar, Wine Bar and Brasserie
Food served all day .... till very late!!
We have changing facilities available,
by arrangement, for golfing parties.

*Morning tea/coffee. Changing
facilities for golf parties.
Lunch or evening dinner.
Wide selection of food and wine.*

Please phone for special rates.
Telephone: 0620 842008
East Links Road, Gullane.
Props: Guy and Brenda Campanile

TO ASSIST WITH
YOUR BOOKINGS
OR ENQUIRIES
YOU WILL FIND IT
HELPFUL TO
MENTION THIS

Pastime Publications Guide

WE'VE MORE THAN OUR SHARE OF SCOTLAND'S GREAT COURSES.

Speak the names out loud. It's like reading a roll call of Scotland's historic courses.

Muirfield, the distinguished Open venue. **Luffness, Gullane, Dunbar**—all, championship qualifying courses. **The West Links** of North Berwick, with its never-to-be forgotten fifteenth hole.

We've sixteen courses in all, a short distance from each other. Courses that many people would give their eye teeth to play. Happily, we're asking for no such thing. A phone call will do.

East Lothian

For your free brochure, details of accommodation and packages, call **0368 63353** or write to: Dept. SG East Lothian Tourist Board, 143 High Street, Dunbar, East Lothian, EH42 1ES

"WE MUST GO BACK TO SCOTLAND....."
By Donald Ford

The American on his annual golfing holiday in Scotland had a particularly bad day. He had hacked, duffed and topped his way around 16 holes of the Carnoustie Championship Course, and it was no surprise to anyone when he again topped his drive on the 17th into the first stretch of the Barry Burn. "With my luck today, Caddy" he said "I would probably drown if I went in after the ball."

Despite 3.5 hours and goodness knows how many extra miles of leg work, the caddy's reply was typically quick and pertinent.

"Ye neednae bother aboot droonin', sir" came the considered reply "ye couldnae keep yer heid doon lang enough!"

Whether true or not, the story epitomises one of the problems of golf in Scotland. Very near the beginning of any of the countless books on how to play golf, the learner is told to keep his head down. A critical instruction - but if you are golfing in Scotland don't let it stay down too long - you are likely to miss some of the most beautiful and spectacular scenery anywhere in the world.

There can be few countries where the landscape changes as quickly or as dramatically as Scotland. From the rolling hills of the Border country, up the magnificent south-west coastline with spectacular views of the Firth of Clyde and the Islands beyond; from the courses in the heart of Edinburgh with panoramic views over the city and the Firth of Forth to the Links of Gullane, Muirfield, North Berwick and Dunbar; through the myriad of courses peppering the Forth and Clyde Valley, into

Fife, where it is not hard to imagine that golf courses came first and towns came second; across the lovely Ochil Hills to Gleneagles, Perthshire and east into Angus; the gorgeous Trossachs country (literally translated 'Trossachs' means 'bristling' - you have to see it to understand it); north-east into the valley of the River Dee with magnificent woodlands and spectacular hills; into the Spey Valley with a smattering of courses which without exception command wonderful vistas of the Cairngorms (as well as being a real test of golf); from Aberdeenshire north to the coast and then westward to Inverness, where some of the best links courses in the country are to be found in some of the most beautiful locations; the choice for the visiting golfer is mouthwatering - the variety is endless.

It is impossible to do justice to the 'Home of Golf' in the space available but we will do our best over the next few pages to whet your appetite and encourage a telephone call to your travel agent. If you have golfed in Scotland before you will know what I am talking about and I know you will be back again. If you haven't been then try to make it in 1994. It's a pretty fair bet that at one point or another during your golfing experience in Scotland you will say "we must come back again...."

I am grateful to Dougie Donnelly and John Chillas for their excellent and colourful contributions and to David Huish, Jim Farmer and of course, Bernard Gallacher for helping to compile "The Best 18 Holes in Scotland". We all hope that you will be here in 1994, that you enjoy your golf, and most important - that you resolve to come again.

THE BORDERS & THE SOUTH-EAST
by Donald Ford

Ladies' Medal Day at Melrose.

The Border counties and south east coastline of Scotland probably have to admit that they do not possess any well known names among Scottish golf courses. What they lack in reputation, however, is amply compensated by the pleasures of playing on any of the lovely courses which nestle among the rolling border hills, valleys of Tweed, Cheviot and Ettrick Water or the more gentle pastureland of Berwickshire with its spectacular coastline. Golf is different in the Borders - it is unhurried (try hurrying up the 9th, 10th and 11th at Galashiels for example - 3 corkers in a row on the west facing slopes of a beautifully maintained course). In a civilised world where we are constantly told that personal standards and behaviour are declining, how lovely it is to discover that Border folk still trust you enough to put green fees in a collection box. Add to that the fact that you

may have the opportunity in one day to play 36 holes on four different golf courses within shouting distance of each other (each with its own little characteristics) and you may understand why this region of Scotland is blessed year after year with returning golfers from all over the world.

As I have often said elsewhere in this editorial it is impossible not to offend some clubs by being unable to give them the space which their individual qualities merit. Nowhere is this statement more appropriate than the Borders. The fact that there are no internationally acclaimed courses seems only to encourage greenkeepers to make their little corner of the world even more attractive. Cynics would say that 9 hole courses cut out of hillsides or laid through heather or strung along a river valley are easy to keep anyway as there is not much you can do with them - how wrong they

The St. Boswells Course at its idyllic best.

would be and how unfair would be their cynicism.

From the lovely 18 hole course at Moffat to the west of the region, all the way across the 40 miles or so to Eyemouth on the Berwickshire coast, a string of carefully kept, and at times, spectacularly beautiful courses will welcome visitors as will some of the nicest people in Scotland. The same pride and enthusiasm which grips the followers of rugby (the Borders' traditional sport) manifests itself among the members of all the golf clubs in their determination to make visiting golfers welcome and to try to ensure when these visitors go home that their course is talked about more than the others.

The town of Moffat, sitting on the western edge of the Southern Uplands, and only a few minutes south of the spectacular Devils Beeftub has a most enjoyable course, typical of those to be found in the area; the town itself thrives on visitors with a lovely broad high street, excellent shops and a succession of first class eating establishments. Away from the main street you will find some of the loveliest little cottages and features in any of the border towns.

South-east of Moffat, with England only a few miles away, there is a little clutch of courses: Hawick, Langholm and Newcastleton.

(The golfing visitor to the Borders will inevitably see a great deal of sheep on his travels; the skills of the Border sheep farmers are renowned world wide. Border folk will tell you that hundreds of years ago when the Scots and the English waged constant wars between each other across the Border hills, a Scottish raiding party decided to invade the North of England and steal their women. Having crossed the border, the Scots took one look at the women and came back with the sheep!)

DUMFRIES AND GALLOWAY

The most southerly region in Scotland, Dumfries and Galloway, is often bypassed - indeed ignored - in any examination of golf in Scotland. To be guilty of such an omission is to make a great mistake because some tremendous golf is available, from the superb Powfoot club at Annan at the eastern end of the area to Portpatrick on the west coast of Wigtownshire which has been acclaimed by "Golf World" as the best holiday course in the south of Scotland.

The fast flowing tides of the Solway Firth, which separate Scotland from England, wash the southern shores of the region, and the spectacular Southerness club which overlooks the Firth is fast obtaining the credit which its wonderful links deserve. This is a tremendous golf course which will thoroughly test your game or provide superb entertainment, whichever of these is your goal. Be warned, however. The straight drive is essential.

Staying on the coastline and moving westwards, Kirkcudbright celebrated its centenary in 1993 and while the course is a shortish test of golf, some uphill holes, as usual, make distances deceptive. A hard working committee has made this a most attractive venue for the golfing visitor.

Inland, towards the eastern end of Dumfries and Galloway, the 9 holes at Lochmaben and the newly constructed Lockerbie course (18 holes - SSS 66) offer first class sport, while the Dumfries and County club is probably one of the best known in the region; a first class test of golf which hosts many championships and is an excellent 18 holes at just under 6,000 yards.

Castle Douglas and Dalbeattie each has a 9 hole layout and while visitors are welcome all year round at Castle Douglas without reservation, check the position at Dalbeattie in advance to ensure availability. The New Galloway club also has a 9-hole course to complete an attractive trio for, perhaps, "A Three in a Day" adventure. Continuing our journey west, futher 9-hole courses at New Galloway, Newton Stewart and Wigtown provide excellent stopping off points, some two-thirds of the way towards the Galloway Peninsula, but you are likely to find the greatest celebrations in 1994 at Glenluce where the Wigtownshire County club celebrates its centenary. This again is an excellent golf course, whose 5,700 yards or thereby will give you a real test.

The most southerly golf course on the Scottish mainland, St. Medan at Port William, is a lovely holiday course. A pleasant 4,400 yards (par 64) with glorious views across the Mull of Galloway and down to the Isle of Man.

Our journey to the west finishes at the Rinns of Galloway where two fine golf courses are available. The Stranraer course which overlooks Loch Ryan is a testing 6,300 yards or thereby (SSS 71), while the Dunskey club at Portpatrick enjoys a tremendous and deserved reputation for its golf course and its welcome to visitors - you are well advised to book in advance of holiday or casual visits. The course is beautifully located on the west coast of the Mull of Galloway and on clear days you can see across the North Channel to the Irish coast, the mountains of Mourne and, despite being the furthest point from the crossing point on the Scottish border, is certainly well worth the trip if you can make it.

This area of Scotland is not renowned for providing world famous golfing venues - there are few "Household Names" which would trip easily off the tongues of potential visitors. Nevertheless, a most pleasant part of Scotland offers some superb golf, with a fine mix of links and parkland to cater for all tastes.

STRATHCLYDE

a. City of Glasgow

The population of Glasgow, at just over 1 million, is more than double that of its great rival Edinburgh but it occupies an area not a great deal greater than Edinburgh, has traditionally been much more industrialised and heavily populated, one result of which is that there has been much less room for laying out golf courses; the choice is limited within the city boundaries therefore.

Nevertheless among those within a few minutes of the motorway network which now snakes its way through the heart of the city there are several courses which will adequately fulfil the needs of the visitor. Of these, Haggs Castle is one of the most attractive, but is a testing 6,464 yards (SSS 71) and visitors require introduction to obtain a round.

Cathkin Braes, home course of that great Scottish comedian Andy Cameron, is another excellent course, as is Cowglen, on the west side of the city. Just outside the western boundary lies Renfrew, which, at 6,818 yards (SSS 73) will sort out your long iron play for you!

On the southern boundaries of the city, in the Newton Mearns area, Whitehills and East Renfrewshire are each superb clubs of the highest quality, both on and off the course. Cochrane Castle in Johnstone welcomes visitors to enjoy a course of 6,226 yards (SSS 70) as does Elderslie, which at 6,031 yards has a standard scratch score of 69.

There are also several publicly owned courses in the city of which Deaconsbank and Lethamhill are perhaps the pick.

On the eastern side of the city, there really is superb golf available. Bishopbriggs provides 2 courses; the first of that name, a 6,041 yards (SSS 69) challenge; while just a mile away on the Cadder Road and across the Forth and Clyde Canal, Cawdor offers 2 courses - the larger of which, at 6,244 yards is an extremely challenging 18 holes - to be frank the Keir Course is not far behind it but slightly less demanding.

Just across the hill lies Lenzie (where on a charity event many years ago I had perhaps my worst round ever in public!) and just a little further out, the 6,042 yard Hayston Course at Kirkintilloch will also prove a daunting challenge. The Kirkintilloch Club itself is also nearby should you be unlucky with advanced bookings at Haystoun.

Other courses around the edge of the city which should not be ignored include Kilmacolm, Ranfurly Castle, Caldwell, Bonnyton (Eaglesham) and the Gleddoch Club at Langbank - all of these to the west of the city, while to the south east, Bothwell Castle in Uddingston, and a little further out, East Kilbride are superb courses with the latter especially, at 6,384 yards, a hard test.

Still on the eastern side of the town Coatbridge offers 2 courses the first of the same name, but the second, Drumpellier, by far the better known and a superb parkland course with a standard scratch score of 70.

b. Around Glasgow

As you leave the built up areas behind you, the opportunities for golf in more rural surroundings, but still within striking distance of the city, simply multiply. Not in any order of preference nor in any geographical pattern, we will start to the north of the city at Milngavie and Bearsden. Between them these 2 commuter towns offer 7 courses with the Bearsden Club itself being the odd man out in offering a 9 hole layout.

Both Windyhill and Douglas Park Clubs welcome visitors by prior arrangement and

Hilton Park, just north of Milngavie, boasts two superb courses; this shot is of the par 4 first hole on the 'Allander'.

Please mention this Pastime Publications guide. 45

the same situation applies at Hilton Park and Dougalston in Milngavie; the Milngavie Club itself welcomes visitors if they are introduced by a member.

There can be few courses around the city of Glasgow which offer such spectacular scenery as the Allander and Hilton Park Courses, set in rolling parkland on the western fringe of the Campsie Fells. Both are tremendous tests of golf and have wonderful views south to the city and north to Dumgoyne and the Loch Lomond area. If you have problems getting a game on any of these courses, then Lennoxtown and Kilsyth, just along the Campsies, are only a few minutes drive away, or a visit to Cumbernauld may well be worth your while.

Here, the Westerwood Course (designed by Severiano Ballasteros) is causing a lot of interest and at 6,721 yards demands the best of you. The Palacerigg Course is also available in the town and again is a stern test with a standard scratch score of 71. The nearby course at Dullatur welcomes visitors (apart from one or two days - check before you go) and Lanark offers the choice of an 18 hole and 9 hole course, with the longer of the 2 having a standard scratch score of 71. A lovely 18 hole layout at Carnwath with superb views south to Tinto and the beginning of the Southern Uplands, is only a ten minutes away and is in magnificent order.

To the west of the area, Helensburgh, Port Glasgow and Gourock welcome visitors Monday to Friday and the Greenock Golf Club proudly offers 27 holes to visitors, but only on Tuesdays, Thursdays and Sundays. Dumbarton provides excellent golf at the Cardross Club, a testing 18 holes which in 1992 hosted the Scottish Professional Championship, won by Paul Lawrie, a young Scot who performed magnificently in the 1993 Open at Sandwich.

Drymen, a lovely little town of some 12 miles north east of the city, offers the magnificence of Buchanan Castle or the more modest Strathendrick 9 hole course, provided you are accompanied by a member.

Plenty choice, therefore, exists within 30 or 45 minutes from the city centre and the biggest problem which will confront the visitor to this part of the country will be in deciding which courses to leave out. Still, you can always come back again!

c. The rest of Strathclyde

The Region of Strathclyde is, without putting too fine a point on it, absolutely enormous. It stretches from Mull and Oban in the North West to the Southern shores of Ayrshire to the South West and it is probably unfair on visitors who are looking for guidance on where to play golf to include areas so far apart as Oban and Turnberry - perhaps 130 miles separate the two.

We will start on the Ayrshire coast which is steeped in golf and has one magnificent course after another along its shores. Prestwick, Troon and Turnberry are legends, of course, and need no further superlatives from me, except to remind you that the town of Prestwick has three courses officially within its boundary. Turnberry offers the Ailsa and Arran courses and if you play to handicap on any of these five (especially if the west wind blows!) you have played extremely well. Turnberry especially, on a summer's day, is sport at its glorious best with fabulous views across the Clyde to Ailsa Craig and Arran - in fact all the courses on this stretch of coastline enjoy wonderful views.

Tacked on the south of Prestwick there is Troon, where the Royal Troon Club hosts the Open Championship but where also you can find three publicly owned courses: Lochside, Darley and Fullerton. Also in Troon is the Barassie Course (known

The 1st green at Lamlash on the Isle of Arran.

officially as the Kilmarnock Golf Club - don't get confused) while just a few miles to the north the lovely course at Glasgow Gailes (just outside Irvine) and the 2 Irvine courses themselves (Bogside and Ravenspark) both welcome visitors and are first class.

Visitors are welcome between Mondays and Fridays at West Kilbride, a testing 6,247 yards (SSS 70) and Largs offers glorious views of the Isle of Cumbrae from its 18 holes (SSS 70).

Just a few miles up the road, at Skelmorlie, there is a very pleasant 13 hole course where male domination of the clubhouse is not now so obvious, as ladies may choose to become full members by paying the equivalent of the full "Male Playing Membership Fee". 2 ladies now sit on the general committee.

Moving southwards again, Ayr offers the well-known Belleisle course (SSS 71) or the publicly owned Dalmilling Course and although there is a fair distance to travel down to Girvan (some 5 miles South of Turnberry) it would be well worth the visit as this lovely little course (SSS 65) has spectacular views over the Clyde to Ailsa Craig.

If the coastline clubs in Ayrshire steal most of the limelight, it should take nothing away from others inland, particularly the wonderfully-named "Loudoun Gowf Club", Beith, Kilmarock, Lochwinnoch and Strathaven Courses further east, and away from the headlines of the Ayrshire Clubs, Lesmahagow (on the M74 heading South) offers a testing par 72 course at Holland Bush which, apart from offering lovely scenery round about, now also sports a new £100,000 clubhouse. The presence of hills, ditches and trees is testament to the amount of money spent by Clydesdale District Council on this excellent golfing facility.

While on the subject of public courses, it is worth mentioning that Kyle & Carrick

District boast that over half a million rounds are played on the public courses in Ayrshire each year (with the aforementioned Ayr Belleisle The Flagship), while Seafield, which lies within the bounds of the old Ayr Racecourse is an interesting mixture of parkland and links and for the less serious golfer Dalmilling, Lochgreen and Maybole would be ideal choices. Information on all these is available from the appropriate council offices.

The Isle of Arran, the Cowal Peninsula, and Islay offer spectacular and unforgettable settings for golfing visitors. Dougie Donnelly has made ample reference to Arran in his own contribution - I will merely add that Shiskine - an extremely testing 12 holes despite being relatively short, and Corrie (near Sannox on the eastern side of the Island) are quite simply gorgeous venues for the visiting golfer; and if there is a better view in Scotland than that of Holy Island from behind the first green at Lamlash, I have yet to find it - mind boggling landscape.

The Cowal Peninsula is not so ruggedly beautiful, but in Dunoon offers a lovely centre for holidaymakers and a tremendous golf course (Cowal) which winds up, down and around the hillside to the northwest of the town offering spectacular views across the Clyde to Gourock, down to the Ayrshire coast, and (just by the way) is a very hard test of golf at 6,251 yards with a par of 70. (If there is a harder par 4 on a Scottish score card than the 4th which goes steeply uphill, invariably into the prevailing west wind, and if that wasn't enough, has an almost right-angled bend to an invisible green, I haven't found it!) Elsewhere on the Peninsula the little 9 hole heathland course at Tighnabruaich offers wonderful views of the Kyles of Bute and 9 hole courses at Innellan and Blairmore also welcome visitors - they are pleasurable rather than demanding courses.

The Isle of Bute offers 2 courses at Rothesay. The main course is a pleasurable 18 holes (5,370 yards) while Port Bannatyne is a 13 hole course with a standard scratch score of 63. There is also a 9 hole course at Kingarth which should not cause you too many problems over its 2,400 yards.

For those holidaymakers who are lucky enough to be even further west, Dunaverty, on the very southern tip of the Kintyre Peninsula is the home course of Belle Robertson, one of Scotland's greatest ever lady golfers. While seven par 3s, on the face of it, make this a fairly comfortable 4,799 yards, the aptly named "Cemetery" - a 446 yard par 5 - will bring you back down to earth with a bump. It just had to be the 13th hole with a name like that!

Campbeltown itself sports 2 courses at Machrihanish, one 18 hole and one 9 hole and visitors are welcome all week. Completing our tour of this lovely part of South-West Scotland, Carradale, Tarbert and Lochgilphead each offer a 9 hole course.

Islay is renowned for its malt whisky and if your vision isn't too badly impaired the morning after, Machrie Golf Club will welcome you at Port Ellen. This is, quite simply, golf at its most idyllic on one of Scotland's most romantic islands with the opportunity of witnessing sunsets more spectacular than anything in the northern hemisphere (and that has nothing to do with whisky!)

The northern part of Strathclyde is not well off for golf courses but you will thoroughly enjoy a round at Glencruitten, in Oban, which has a liberal sprinkling of par 3s, hidden greens, blind approach shots, etc. etc. Typical highland hospitality awaits you in the clubhouse however, and the bustling tourist town of Oban has lots to offer all the family. These latter facilities include superb ferry services to Mull, in particular, and the lovely Tobermory course (9 holes, SSS 64) will provide excellent sport for you. To the south east of the island Craignure also offers a 9 hole challenge (SSS 64) but, irrespective of the quality of the golf, you are again guaranteed memorable sport in magnificent surroundings and, of course, the warmest possible welcome from some of the most hospitable folks in Scotland.

Before closing off Strathclyde it would be unfair not to mention the efforts of members of the Vaul Club at Scarinish on the Isle of Tiree - miles from the mainland but still they enjoy their sport and you are assured of a warm welcome if you arrive there with your clubs!

Quite deliberately, I have left to the very end of this section The Loch Lomond Country Club development at Luss on the west shore of Loch Lomond. Tom Weiskopf has been responsible for designing a quite magnificent parkland course which will use Rossdhu House, once renovated, as its headquarters, and amateurs and professionals alike are raving about the potential of this superb test of golf. Using the natural contours of the land, the wonderful and varied species of trees which abound, and positioning the most massive and terrifying bunkers all over the place (sand alone set the developers back £100,000) Weiskopf has created a golf course which threatens to be one of the top six in Scotland when all facilities are complete. Try to find time for a round - a tremendous course, a great challenge to your ability, and a situation unparalleled for scenery - no one could possibly wish for more.

Former Open Champion Tom Weiskopf designed the lovely Loch Lomond Course (near Luss) where huge bunkers are everywhere! This one guards the green at the short 8th.

Please mention this Pastime Publications guide.

FIFE

W hen you catch sight of the towers and spires on your approach to St. Andrews and the familiar shape of the Old Course Hotel and then the Royal and Ancient Clubhouse comes into view, you will feel, at the very least, a tingle of excitement. You can almost touch the atmosphere which grips the old Fife town; very few, if any, of the famous names which have graced these Old Links over the last 120 years or so have failed to be moved by the magnetism of the home of golf. In the passage of time, whatever changes lie ahead in this wonderful game of golf, St. Andrews will always be king; the others are only pretenders.

Bernard Gallacher now professional at Wentworth and Captain of the European Ryder Cup team has said that there is no other 1st tee in the world which can generate, even remotely, the atmosphere of the 1st on the Old Course on the opening morning of an Open Championship. I rest my case. If you think I am playing with words, come and feel it for yourself.

St. Andrews is rightly the golfing capital of Scotland and of Fife itself but do not for a minute allow that to distract you from the wonderful courses scattered throughout this old county which almost dare you to challenge them. Scarcely have you left the Forth Road Bridge behind you, than the three Dunfermline courses are waiting for you; Pitreavie on the main approach road to the town and the Dunfermline Course (in Crossford around a mile to the west of the town) which features the old castle. Within part of its facilities are excellent parkland courses which will get your golfing holiday in Fife off to a good start.

Moving eastwards to the coast the lovely little town of Aberdour offers a magnificent 18 hole course of parkland (despite its proximity to the sea); at 5,460 yards and with a liberal sprinkling of par 3's it is an ideal "2 rounds in a day" course with spectacular views, down southwards across the Firth of Forth to the city of Edinburgh.

Just a couple of miles up the coast lies Burntisland, another lovely 18 holes with a standard scratch of 69, very friendly members and excellent hospitality. The much shorter but still challenging Kinghorn is next, before the old linoleum-making town of Kirkcaldy offers you the choice of the Kirkcaldy Club in Balwearie Road or Dunnikier Park to the north of the town.

The fast Kirkcaldy/Glenrothes Link Road will have you at the clubhouse in Glenrothes in about 10 minutes. The 5,984 yard course, developed when the new town was built in the late 1960's has a standard scratch score of 71 and will give your game a hard examination. A couple of miles to the east on the wonderful Balbirnie Park Estate, is the beautiful parkland course of the same name which in the height of summer is absolutely magnificent. Now reaching its best after recent development you will enjoy the 6,400 yards which demand a more than average performance with your long irons.

To complete this little trip through the heart of Fife the superb heathland of Ladybank is but a further 10 minutes up the Dundee Road. An open qualifying course (6,641 yards) with a standard scratch of 72 you will love the individuality of the tree-lined holes and woe betide you if you have one of these days when you cannot hit the ball straight.

If it is links golf which you are after, however, then the stretch of coastline from Leven, round the East Neuk of Fife to St. Andrews will provide the sternest of tests but at the same time offer links golf at its best. Like Ladybank, Leven and Lundin

Inchcolm Abbey and the Firth of Forth are regularly in view from the lush fairways of Aberdour; this shot looks down on the 3rd green.

Please mention this Pastime Publications guide

Links both feature as open championship qualifying courses; both are almost identical in length and as you putt out on the 2nd green at Leven you can shake hands across the wall with those who have just completed the 4th on Lundin Links.

Both are great seaside courses demanding straight driving, excellent iron play, and of course, one of the major ingredients of your round will be traditional Scottish "bump & run". (For lady golfers in the company the Lundin Ladies' Club offers a beautiful little 9 hole course of 2,365 yards, with the old standing stones a feature, and the lump of Largo Law overlooking the proceedings).

Just a few miles up the road, the two Elie courses await you: Earlsferry is southern-most of the two but is not as well known as its neighbour at the golf house club in Elie itself, again an open championship qualifying course with a standard scratch of 70 and an extremely testing 6,241 yards of enjoyable but testing golf in the ever-present east coast winds.

Anstruther, yet another of the seemingly never-ending Fife fishing villages which have, so sadly, lost the hustle and bustle of the once thriving fishing industry on the East Coast, has a pleasant little 9 hole course of some 2,500 yards to test you out alongside the shore to the south of the town.

Last in line of these idylic seaside courses in Fife is the Balcomie Club on Fifeness, a couple of miles north of Crail. This is a wonderful golfing experience with a combination of links and parkland on the very tip of Fife. At 5,720 yards (standard scratch 68) it appears not, on the face of it to be the greatest test of your golf; don't believe it for a minute! You will never play this course without, at the very least, a sea breeze blowing and if the wind really blows you will be very hard pushed to play to handicap - it's a bit of a tiger of a course.

If you tire at all of the St. Andrews courses or fancy a change of scenery then Scotscraig at Tayport (a few miles north-west of St. Andrews) has a superb course which has again been used for open qualifying with a standard scratch of 71.

The 4th green at Lundin Links.

An early morning shot at 'The Home of Golf' features the flag at the 17th (Road Hole) on the Old Course.

CENTRAL REGION

The clubs and courses in the heart of the Forth valley are not accustomed to having their praises sung, nor to grabbing the headlines. Few, if any, of the majors which take place in Scotland find their way here. True, there are no tigerish links nor cunningly conceived parkland fairways which might encourage the powers-that-be to bring a big tournament to the area.

However, try telling members of Glenbervie, Stirling, Grangemouth, to name but three, that their courses are not of championship standard and you will be on the receiving end of some well-deserved abuse. I have never played to handicap at Glenbervie (what a very difficult finish!) The long Grangemouth course is vastly underrated and despite having the benefit of a 2-handicap partner, I have twice been on the receiving end of thrashings from John Chillas and a colleague in recent seasons at Stirling. It is superbly laid out on an escarpment to the west of the castle, with magnificent views of the old town, but more important, a very challenging 6,409 yards - if you get par at the first hole, you deserve to do well.

Glenbervie, now the home course of John Chillas and formerly of that legend of Scottish golf John Panton, is quite simply superb. John Chillas himself, as well as being one of the best tournament pros. in Scotland, is also an excellent tutor, and if you have problems with your swing the probability is that he will have the problem quickly solved and the correct medicine prescribed. But to the course itself; at just over 6,400 yards (SSS 71) it is an extremely challenging 18 holes with long par 4's demanding accurate driving and iron play and big greens to put your putting through the mill as well. Without a doubt, one of the best courses in Central Scotland.

Only a mile away you are sure of a warm welcome at either of the two Falkirk courses - the Tryst is very flat but at just over 6,000 yards again demands a lot of accuracy off the tee; Falkirk Carmuirs in the Camelon district of Falkirk is one of the most hospitable in the district. It has a standard scratch score of 69 like its near neighbour, but is marginally longer and has more varied contours than the Tryst. As an afterthought I can personally vouch for the quality of the catering!

Along the foothills of the Ochils there is a string of most attractive courses of which Schaw Park at Sauchie is probably the pick but that is in no way meant to be disrespectful to the others. Starting from the western edge of the Ochils at Bridge of Allan and moving east through Alloa, Alva, Tillicoultry and Dollar you will enjoy the challenge offered by the Heathland at the foot of the Ochils; in particular, if you can find a more precipitous tee shot than that at the second (par 3) at Dollar, I would be interested to hear about it. All are great sport and have fine views of the hills and the Forth Valley. The course at Tulliallan on the north side of the Forth at Kincardine enjoys an excellent reputation and if you can't master the 6,000 yards or thereby, you can always pop next door to get some help at the Police College.

At the western end of the region lies the lovely little town of Dunblane and while the family enjoys the little shops and explores the beautiful cathedral, you can make yourself useful on the 5,800 yards (SSS 68) of the Dunblane New Club, another excellent course which is very popular for outings although catering has be be booked in advance.

Autumn begins to tint the trees which are such a feature of the superb Glenbervie Course; this oak is behind the 13th green.

CITY OF EDINBURGH
EAST LOTHIAN, MIDLOTHIAN & WEST LOTHIAN

Putting out on the 17th at Swanston with fine views of the City of Edinburgh.

The city of Edinburgh has some 20 courses awaiting the visitor, and basically there is something for everyone. For those who don't know the city, let us get one thing clear right away, Edinburgh has hills. If you enjoy putting your wits against slopes, stiff breezes and enjoy the odd blind approach to a green, then try Torphin Hill, Swanston, The Merchants or Lothianburn and you won't be disappointed.

Occupying similar positions on the hills within the city boundaries, which offer splendid views over Scotland's capital, are the Braid Hills courses (superb tests of golf) Mortonhall, Craigmillar Park, Murrayfield and Ravelston (the latter a lovely little 9-holer which you can scoot round in an hour and half comfortably). Bruntsfield, Royal Burgess, Duddingston, Baberton and Ratho Park offer quite magnificent parkland courses and will all test the low handicapper in one way or another.

The short 13th. At tree-lined Ratho Park.

At the time of writing these courses are all in superb condition; in particular Ratho Park (which, with the multitude of trees in and around it is an oasis from the hustle and bustle of the city), could easily be mistaken for Augusta with white sand in bunkers, sea shells on paths and magnificent manicuring of the course and its surrounds.

Just a stone's throw from Ratho Park, and almost within the city boundaries, lies Dalmahoy Golf & Country Club, which in 1992 was the scene of the European Ladies' victory over USA in the Solheim Cup. Dalmahoy also will host the Scottish Professional Championship for the next 3 years and is a splendid and at times exacting course which demands excellent long iron play if a decent score is to be achieved.

The "Big Two" on the north-west side of the city: Royal Burgess and Bruntsfield Links, exude class, both in terms of the golf courses themselves and in the clubhouse facilities offered - if you are lucky enough to get a game on either of these courses, it is an experience you won't forget.

Not to mention Duddingston, Prestonfield, Baberton and Kingsknowe would be remiss; beautiful courses with the friendliest of welcomes from members and clubhouse staff. And talking about friendly atmospheres you will go a long way to find more hospitable receptions than those at Carrick Knowe or Silverknowes, the latter quietly positioned on the shores of the Forth, just east of Cramond, and a fine test of golf for the visitor, especially if the wind blows.

The visiting golfers to Lothian Region might well feel spoilt for choice within the city of Edinburgh; what awaits them however, within a 25 mile radius of Princes Street is mindboggling. The offerings on East Lothian's links are legend (Muirfield, Longniddry, Gullane, Luffness and the North Berwick and Dunbar courses will do for starters).

In Midlothian, some 20 minutes from the city centre, take your pick from Broomieknowe (an excellent golf range adjacent); Newbattle, Monktonhall and Royal Musselburgh; Glencorse, just outside Penicuik, and some 15 minutes or so further down the "back of the Pentland Hills" lies West Linton which offers spectacular views of the Pentland Hills to the north and west and the beginning of the Southern Uplands to the south.

West Lothian courses are often looked on as the poor relations of the region but this is being totally unfair to a championship - standard 18 holes at Deer Park, Livingston which is acknowledged as being one of the hardest tests of golf in the area with long par 4's demanding excellent driving and 1st class iron play and an exposed position on the eastern slope of Dechmont Law bringing the inevitable Scottish winds into play again.

Bernard Gallacher's home town course of Bathgate is excellent; some 6 miles to the south near West Calder, is Harburn, dismissed by many as being too far out of the way but which possesses 18 challenging holes of infinite variety. If your round at Harburn isn't up to scratch, you can relax in the beautiful clubhouse (whose £250,000 extension was recently completed - what a meal you can enjoy.)

Pumpherston, on the western boundary of Livingston, has a friendly little 9-holer for the less energetic and remains etched in my memory as hosting the best annual golf dinner I have ever attended.

Moving a little further north, the 18 holes at Linlithgow (which were saved from extinction by a generous 11th hour intervention by the late Mrs. Gina McKinnon, whose family has held for centuries, and continues to hold the recipe for Drambuie) will demand 1st class driving and excellent work around the greens for the

The hunk of the Bass Rock is featured in this shot from the back of the 15th green on the East (Glen) Course.

visitor; it sits on the hillside to the west of the town but is by no means over-strenuous. The par 3 17th is certain to tickle your fancy, if nothing else.

2 miles further north lies the West Lothian course, technically in Central Region, but inhabitants of Bo'ness, the nearest town, would still like to be part of the Lothians. A wonderfully friendly club will make the visitor welcome and the course will offer splendid sport with fantastic views of the Forth Valley - from the Trossachs right down to the 2 Forth Bridges at Queensferry and beyond - thrown in for good measure. If you have time do not miss out the West Lothian courses from your itinerary.

Without doubt, the pulse begins to race and the excitement tingles as you head down the east coast to the links courses, strung along the southern shore of the Firth of Forth and "round the corner" to Dunbar.

The East Lothian skyline is dominated by the extinct volcanic cone of North Berwick Law and the hump of Traprain Law but it is a beautiful part of the country with rich farmland and lovely little villages dotted around.

If Muirfield is the jewel in the crown, having been the scene of many epic open championship battles, it has to be said that you may well have difficulty in getting a game there.

Such disappointment will be overcome when you switch your attention to Gullane (three lovely courses, of which No. 1 is an absolute stinker when the wind blows but is wonderfully laid out and offers spectacular views westwards up the Firth of Forth). The West Course at North Berwick and the East Course at Dunbar epitomise the Scottish links course as they stretch their way west and east respectively along the seashore. Longniddry which has hosted the seniors'

championship is a mixture of links and parkland with a superb layout which demands accurate driving and accurate approach play.

Just 2 miles east of Longniddry, at Aberlady, Kilspindie is an ideal course for 2 rounds in a day. It starts off with a hard par 3, a long par 5 and two par 4's along the beach which are inevitably into a strong west wind and at that stage you wonder (if you are there for the first time) what you have let yourself in for. Thereafter this lovely course demands little exertion from you but club selection can be extremely difficult; I have used an 8 iron and a 3 wood off the tee at the par 3 8th, for example. Hospitality abounds in the little clubhouse and you are guaranteed a 1st class meal in friendly company.

To complete the high quality chain along the East Lothian shore, one must never ignore Luffness - an open championship qualifying course in its own right and the southern neighbour of the Gullane courses. The success or failure of your round here will again be influenced by the wind but also by the wicked placement of little pot bunkers. You will need an introduction to allow a round but it is well worth the effort.

Finally, mention must be made of Haddington, very much the shadow of the more renowned courses on the coast, but a standard scratch score of 70 indicates that this is no pushover. By the way, it is a lovely town too; 5 miles away, the beautiful village of Gifford offers a most enjoyable round on the edge of the Lammermuir Hills.

An abundance of choice within an hour of Scotland's capital offers just about everything for the golfer but the popularity and high levels of membership of most courses makes advance booking desirable.

GRAMPIAN REGION

In terms of size, Grampian Region is very similar to Tayside; when you bring into account, however, that the mass of the Cairngorm mountains, the foothills and the glens through which some of Scotland's loveliest rivers flow take up about 30% of the area, then one understands why there is not an abundance of courses in the region.

That having been said, the quality of those which do exist is, once again, superb. They are fairly comfortably divided into four main areas: the city of Aberdeen, the Dee Valley, the east coast from Stonehaven in the south to Fraserburgh in the north, and the Moray Firth coastline and its hinterland, from MacDuff in the east to Nairn in the west (strictly speaking the latter is in Highlands and Islands region, but with characteristics so like those of the other links courses on this stretch of coastline it is included here.

The city of Aberdeen and the area within five or ten miles offers a first class mix of links and parkland golf, with public courses (King's Links, Bon Accord and Balnagask) also available. High quality, both of layout and appearance, is guaranteed in an area which has been fortunate to remain above the general level of recession which has affected many parts of the country over the last few years.

Custom has it that Aberdeen folk are miserable with their money; take that with a pinch of salt and be assured that it certainly does not apply to the memberships of the various clubs around the city which will make you more than welcome. Murcar, Balgownie and Royal Aberdeen are probably the pick of the clubs although the members of Deeside and Westhill will probably not thank me for saying that! Memberships are growing steadily and advance booking is well-advised.

Just outside the city but within easy reach are Portlethen, Cults, Bucksburn and Cothall, with Bucksburn probably enjoying the greatest reputation of that group. Some ten to twelve miles west of the city Kemnay offers a 9 hole course and Kintore, some two miles to the east, a stern 18 holes of just under 6,000 yards at a very reasonable daily charge. To the north, Old Meldrum has a near 6,000 yards layout; Inverurie is but a stone's throw away, and, to the north west, the course at Ellon was upgraded to 18 holes in 1975. The new first nine has matured significantly over the past few years providing a very good challenge to your golfing skills. An ambitious committee also looks forward to a brand new clubhouse within the next eighteen months.

The tourist routes through Deeside are, not suprisingly, extremely busy during the holiday season as thousands of visitors throng this most delightful part of northern Scotland. The Valley of the Dee is quite beautiful with lovely towns and spectacular scenery throughout the forty to fifty mile course of the river to the North Sea. You will find the golf courses magnificent from the highest 18 hole course on mainland Britain, Braemar in the far west, to Banchory in the east.

Aboyne and Ballater are probably the most popular and heavily played courses along this stretch of countryside, but that should take nothing away from the 9 hole courses at Tarland and Torphins, the former having panoramic views towards Lochnagar and its neighbouring mountains, a difficult upland course but easily walked with a liberal sprinkling of par 3s in its 5,816 yards. This is another part of the country where, irrespective of the quality of your golf, you cannot fail to be enthralled by the

A three-some set off after their drives on the fine parkland course of Duff House Royal.

magnificence all around. Once again I would remind you that this is a very busy part of Grampian region and advance booking of your requirements is well-advised.

The east coast of Aberdeenshire (it is still hard to get away from the old name!) supplies some magnificent links courses with Cruden Bay (where the locals tell me that golf was played as early at 1791) probably the best known and most challenging. The legendary Tom Morris supervised the layout of the course by Thomas Simpson and in 1984 "Golf World" had Cruden Bay in the top forty courses of Britain - perhaps that says it all. Superb views over the Bay of Cruden simply add to the magnificence of this course and you are promised a very stiff challenge on its 6,370 yards (SSS 70). A little

to the south, the 9 holes at Newburgh on the River Ythan will prove a daunting task if the wind blows over its 6,300 yards, while some miles to the north of Cruden Bay you will find a warm welcome at Peterhead, one of the busiest seaports on the Aberdeenshire coastline, indeed one of the busiest in Europe.

Moving to the extreme north of the coast the little par 64 course at Inverallochy is most pleasant and not an energy-sapper, while Fraserburgh at the "top right corner" of the Scottish mainland has a more testing 6,279 yard course (SSS 70).

Scattered at regular intervals along the northern coastline of the region are some of the loveliest little fishing villages in Britain. These should not be missed if you have a

The 18th green and ruined church, Stonehaven with Dunotter Castle in the distance.

day off - and don't forget your camera! Similarly spaced out there are some beautiful golf courses with a mixture of links and parkland (the latter generally found on the cliff tops with spectacular views out over the sea) and some real challenging golf for you as well.

Having included Nairn, as the character of the town fits in so well with all of those along this most beautiful stretch of coastline, it is fitting that we should begin our examination of the North Grampian courses here. This is yet another traditional Scottish links course which was created from a wilderness of whins and heather in 1887, with assistance ultimately from Tom Morris and James Braid. The course regularly attracts big tournaments and in 1994 will host the amateur championship. No doubt the magnificent new clubhouse (built in 1990) went a long way towards securing this most prestigious event on the amateur calendar.

The club also offers a less strenuous 9 hole course (the Newton) and a full size practice ground adjacent to the 18th fairway. If you are in this area, Nairn should not be by-passed.

Moving east, the 18 holes at Forres (6,141 yards, SSS 69) is another first class test and the Hopeman Club, on the coast just a few miles from Elgin, is a less-strenuous 5,474 yards but will provide excellent sport. The town of Elgin itself has a superb and testing 6,401 yard layout (SSS 71); a fine course with lots of difficult features make this an excellent, if more strenuous, round of golf.

Moving back to the coast - but only a few miles from Elgin - Lossiemouth offers two excellent 18 hole courses, the "Old" being a really superb links course in yet another perfect example of Scottish links golf. If you are not a "bump and run" enthusiast then you will certainly have problems here!

The Spey Bay Club in Fochabers is tailor-made for visitors with the club's Open Tournament in late July/early August providing entertainment every night. The course itself is a 6,064 yard, par 71, and was the home course of the first Labour Prime Minister Ramsay MacDonald, whose trophy, presented to the club in 1929 is still the prize for the Club Champion each year. There are some special packages available through the hotel which feature daily, two day or five day options at very attractive rates - worth serious thought if you will be in this part of the world.

A few miles further east the fishing port of Buckie has two 18 hole courses on offer. Buckpool which stretches west along the coastline and is an excellent, fairly flat 6,257 yards and at the other end of the town, just beyond Portessie, the Strathlene Club lies on the clifftop and stretches eastwards offering parkland golf with lovely views to the Moray Firth - and a beautiful new clubhouse to entertain you afterwards.

Another 10 minutes hop eastwards takes you to Cullen and the start of a succession of quite lovely fishing villages in a 30 mile stretch of this coastline. The course is dramatic, to say the least, and switches from the links alongside the beach at Cullen Bay to high ground above the clifftops; more than a few blind tee shots and very difficult clubbing make this a highly entertaining experience - and the views are stunning.

In contrast with Cullen, the magnificent parkland of Duff House Royal in Banff is splendour personified. Flat land between Duff House (which is absolutely gorgeous) and the banks of the River Deveron just before it enters the sea, has spawned a quite magnificent 18 holes (6,161 yards - SSS 69). In a completely different way, your round here will be as memorable as the one at Cullen or Royal Tarlair - there are some restrictions on playing times however and a handicap certificate is preferred.

Only a five iron or so from the 18th tee at Duff House is the western boundary of the town of MacDuff. A very busy fishing town whose name was made famous through the character of the same name in Shakespeare's "MacBeth"; if neither fishing nor Shakespeare appeals to you, but golf does, then the fantastic stretch of clifftops to the east of the town, where Royal Tarlair awaits you, will entertain you over its 5,866 yards of splendid layout and lush green fairways and will thrill you with wonderful panoramas of towering cliffs falling sheer into the North Sea. Breathtaking stuff!

If you can tear yourself away from the beauty of the Moray Firth and North Sea coastline and the superb sport which the golf courses there will provide for you, a handful of courses just a twenty minute car journey inland are also worthy of attention. Huntly, Keith, Fochabers, Dufftown and Turriff all have excellent 18 hole courses of which Turriff at 6,100 yards or thereby (SSS 69) is possibly the hardest. It has the added bonus of allowing visitors at the weekends provided they start after 10 o'clock in the morning.

Simply because you don't hear the names of these courses on television or read about them in the press very often, do not underestimate or undervalue the sport which they offer. This is a wonderful part of Scotland for golf with the choice of traditional and often frustrating Scottish links and glorious parkland; tremendous sea air to fill your lungs and dramatic scenery to provide the memories - there's not a lot more one could ask for.

TAYSIDE

The grandeur of the exterior of Taymouth Castle dominates this view of the popular Tayside Course of the same name.

W hen the reconstruction of the old Scottish "County" boundaries was planned by Lord Wheatley in 1973, even he could not have imagined that in the creation of Tayside there would be one of the loveliest areas of the country which would contain a wide diversity in countryside, industry and recreation.

As with many other parts of Scotland, rivers play a great part in the added beauty of the region. The Earn, the Tay itself, the Tummel and the two Esks all wend their way to the Firth of Tay or the North Sea through some beautiful countryside. "The Tay, the Tay, the Silvery Tay" (as the notorious Dundee poet McGonagall put it) basically splits the region as it flows from Kenmore on the Eastern bank of beautiful Loch Tay through Aberfeldy, Dunkeld and Perth and widens out to the Firth of Tay, at the city of Dundee.

This area tends to enjoy rather better weather than the western side of the country, indeed the area around the Tay

The Barry Burn much in evidence as it guards the 10th green ('South America') at Carnoustie.

estuary (which includes, obviously, the Northern Fife towns as well) has one of the best sunshine records in Scotland. Nowhere is this more apparent in late July and August than on the links courses of Angus where the fairways burn, and given a kind bounce from the links, you will be driving the ball further than you could possibly imagine!

Lovely scenery and beautiful towns abound in the area. Apart from the city of Dundee, the town of Perth has excellent shops and recreational facilities and is a first class centre to sample the whole region and even perhaps to act as the southern base of

an exploration further north to the Highlands and Grampian region, if you are of such a mind.

Just as St. Andrews was the star of Fife region, so Gleneagles carries the banner for Tayside. (Residents of Carnoustie may not thank me for that comment, but their turn will come later.) I could not possibly add any more adjectives to those which have been used in previous descriptions of Gleneagles. Apart from the supreme quality of the courses (with Jack Nicklaus' recent Monarch Course being added - and from all accounts it is a cracker), the scenery around the courses is simply wonderful. South and west to the north face of the Ochil Hills and Glendevon, northwards towards the southern beginnings of the Grampians, and eastwards down the Earn Valley - wherever you look the views are magnificent. You will be very unlucky (especially in early morning or late evening) not to catch sight of deer, rabbit, grouse, pheasant and a multitude of other examples of the wild life which abounds in the area but you will not see any eagles! Despite its name, Gleneagles is derived from the French word "Aiglise" - a church - and has nothing to do with the feathered variety.

The problem with Gleneagles is that it is very hard to get a game. Nevertheless a visit is worthwhile; the hotel is legend and a walk across the Kings or Queens course, even if you don't have the opportunity to have a game, will make it easier to understand why so many people have been enraptured by Gleneagles over the years.

Golf abounds in the area around Gleneagles with Crieff perhaps the pick of the nearest courses. That takes nothing away from a lovely heathland course at Muckhart just through Glendevon to the south (some 6 or 7 miles away); the course which adjoins Gleneagles at Auchterarder is very pleasant and has similar spectacular views; Comrie and St. Fillans, the latter at the eastern end of lovely Loch Earn, offer two very attractive 9 hole courses as does the village of Dunning on the main Perth to Stirling Road, and Milnathort, just a few miles from Loch Leven.

Many of the Scottish regions are now offering a "Round Robin" season ticket and Tayside is no exception. This offers cut price golf at any one of seven or eight courses in the area and is worth enquiring about at your local travel agent.

Moving to the north west of the region, the gorgeous little town of Killin on the western bank of Loch Tay and famous for the Falls of Dochart, offers a very attractive 9 hole golf course with stunning views down the Loch, and the little town of Kenmore, similarly situated, but at the eastern end of the Loch now has two courses to offer the visitor. The more well known is that of Taymouth Castle which is magnificently laid out in parkland around a typical old Scottish baronial home, among wooded hillsides to the north and south and on the very banks of the Tay as it begins its journey to the North Sea. In the village itself the recent development of a leisure centre, with a wide variety of sport and entertainment for all the family, has been created by the Menzies family and a very attractive 9 hole course undulating around the valley will provide excellent relaxation - beginners and children are not allowed on the course unless accompanied by an adult.

Aberfeldy, just a few miles to the east, Blair Atholl, at the very north of the region and Glenshee (the latter just a few miles from one of Scotland's top winter ski resorts) all offer 9 holes as does the Little Club at Strathtay, by Aberfeldy - once again beautiful countryside all around. The same can be said about the lovely 9 hole course at Dunkeld and just a few miles up the A9 the busy tourist town of Pitlochry which has so much to offer visitors to the area, provides a superb 18 holes stretching to 5,811 yds - no one who plays this course in the right weather will come off the 18th green disappointed.

The town of Perth offers Craigiehill, situated on rising ground to the south west of the town with lovely views over the town centre, Valley of the Tay, and Kinnoull Hill, and the famous King James VI Club lies on Moncrieff Island in the river itself, is very flat, but a testing 18 holes with a standard scratch 68.

The main Perth to Aberdeen road which

Warm sunshine bathes the 7th fairway at Muckhart.

runs between the low Sidlaw Hills to the south and the southern beginnings of the Grampians, very soon takes you to the lovely Tayside towns which lie at the southern ends of the glens of Angus. Blairgowrie, Alyth, Forfar, Kirriemuir, Brechin and Edzell will bring out the very best in you; if the glorious Rosemount Course at Blairgowrie with its magnificent tree-lined fairways is the most renowned of this group, it should not detract from the excellent and difficult challenges of the others. (If there is a harder second shot to judge than that at the 18th at Kirriemuir, with a huge gully in front of the green, a massive bunker, trees on the right and you can't see the bottom of the flag - then I haven't found it yet). The most northerly of this group, at Edzell, is a stiff 6,348 yds with an SSS of 70 - excellent sport - and genial club professional Alistair Webster (one of Scotland's leading pros) will make you more than welcome.

The "City of Discovery" - Dundee - where the old sailing ship lies in Port awaiting thousands more visitors, offers a wide variety in golfing entertainment: from basic public courses to the long and very testing

Downfield Club (over 6,800 yds with an SSS of 73). A lot of very good and very famous golfers have come from this part of the world and it is not coincidence that they have been able to enjoy the combination of superb parkland, such as Downfield, and only half an hour away some of the greatest links golf in the world. Dundonians are justly proud of their city and of many famous sportsmen who have learned the skills of their trades on the various sportsfields of Dundee; they are a knowledgeable bunch and not withstanding their fierce pride in their city welcome visitors with open arms.

Within 25 minutes of Dundee City Centre lie 6 courses which could fill a fortnight's holiday and still leave you wondering why a good score on any of them is so elusive. The two courses at Monifieth, Panmure, (Barry) and the three Carnoustie courses, (Championship, Burnside and Buddon) are wonderful tests of links golf, hugely enjoyable and in the case of the Championship course at Carnoustie an unforgettable experience as these links are the toughest and longest in Scotland.

Good driving, good long iron play and accuracy on and around the massive greens are all essential if you are looking for a decent score - and that is before we talk about the wind.

The current tragedy of such a great golf course is that the infrastructure around it fails nowadays to cope with the requirements of hosting the Open Championship. At approximately 7,000 yds you will appreciate, if nothing else, the refreshment kiosk behind the 10th green. If the "Medal" Course proves too much for you, don't overlook the Burnside; a wonderful mix of tight fairways, clinging heather, seaside links at their undulating best (or worst) and the Barry Burn thrown in for good measure. Monifieth and Barry have both been used for Open qualifying courses which adequately testifies to their challenges. If that is not enough for you then some 20 miles further up the coast at Montrose you can find the epitomy of seaside golf on yet another links course of Championship stature bounded on one side by the dunes and beach and on the other by the old town of Montrose.

If you are not thoroughly exhausted by the breathtaking (in more ways than one) golf around Tayside region, then Letham Grange, some 4 miles north of Arbroath, offers a superb course, opened in 1987 by the late Sir Henry Cotton and host, among other things, to Peter Alliss' television series, "Play Better Golf". Justifiably described as "another Augusta" the par 73, 6,614 yd course incorporates narrow tree-lined fairways, lakes and lovely undulating parkland and is a real test of golf. If that is still not enough, pop down to Arbroath itself and enjoy the 18 holes of the Elliot Course on the links to the west side of the town; publicly owned but with very reasonable charges for an extremely pleasant course.

It is impossible for the golfer not to find something to suit him (or her) somewhere around Tayside region. If you have the desire to go home and boast about the greatest championship links in the world, they await you on the Angus coast. If you want to add even more stories to the legends of Gleneagles you have no problem. If you want leisurely, uncluttered, and comfortable rounds amidst wonderful scenery, with the need to break course records secondary, there are courses in abundance here. A final word of advice, - Don't forget your camera!

HIGHLANDS & ISLANDS

We begin our visit to the largest area on our Golf Itinerary on the Perth to Inverness highway, "The A9 Corridor" which is the main access route to Inverness, the far north and the spectacular north west - where you will find the most wonderful scenery in Britain.

The Valley of the Tilt leads you through Tayside to the little town of Blair Atholl, with its spectacular castle set against a backdrop of mountains and you will enjoy thoroughly the nine-hole course set around the river and the southern edge of the town.

Through the Drumochter Pass and past the much-photographed distillery at Dalwhinnie, you are now plunging into the real highlands and the Spey Valley provides a lovely contrast to the grandeur and, sometimes, threatening appearance of the mountains.

The Newtonmore Course lies on the floor of the Spey Valley and provides an excellent 18 holes which will fully satisfy either the seious or recreational golfer. Just a few miles up the road, and enjoying a superb position on the rising ground to the west of the town, the 18 hole course at Kingussie similarly offers a splendid golf course in an excellent and varied layout; if you happen to have an off day, then don't worry - the magnificent views across the Spey Valley to the Cairngorms will more than compensate. It goes without saying that the two towns aforementioned will offer wonderful hospitality in their respective clubhouses to all visitors.

The same applies a little further up the A9 at Boat of Garten where the par 69 (5,837 yards) 18 hole course is a gem. Many problems await you here if your driving is awry, but again the highland atmosphere is wonderful and the welcome in the friendly clubhouse afterwards is warm and generous.

(Incidentally, if the family isn't too happy at dad having yet another round of golf, the Strathspey Railway and its lovely collection of restored steam trains will provide an hour or two of entertainment and a return trip to Aviemore, the Highland centre of Scottish skiing and outdoor pursuits.

Only a golf course yardage away from Boat of Garten, at Carrbridge, there is an extremely pleasant 9-hole course - don't forget to have a look at General Wade's Packhorse Bridge while you are in the village - and if you are still enjoying this part of the world, try a round at Nethy Bridge where the Abernethy Club celebrated its centenary in 1993. A beautifully manicured little course (par 66) is ideal for an early morning round to blow away the cobwebs and will not prove too much of an exertion; another friendly clubhouse with lovely views of the Spey valley and the Cairngorms - well worth a visit.

Finally, in this most scenic part of the highlands try to find time to test out the 18 holes at Grantown-On-Spey, where the 5,631 yard layout (SSS 67) is one of the best in the Highlands and visitors will be welcome all week.

From Inverness, where the local club's 18 hole course (SSS 70) is busy all the year round with visitors and members, all the way up the east coast to Wick, there is golfing available at regular intervals in the towns en route. By far the most famous of these is Royal Dornoch - many leading professionals wish that this magnificent golf course could be lifted and dropped in a part of the United Kingdom where a new accessibility would allow far more tournaments to be played on it; maybe it is fortunate that it enjoys distance from the heavy populations and, therefore, remains a jewel to be admired and enjoyed only by those who are prepared

The view looking down the second fairway of the very attractive Boat of Garten Course.

to make the effort to get there - a wonderful experience.

Dornoch's reputation should not detract in any way from the sport available on another dozen or so of the courses up this coastline. Only 20 minutes or so from Inverness, the 18 holes at Stathpeffer, while only stretching to 4,800 yards or thereby is an excellent base for holiday golf, and courses at Alness, Invergordon and Portmahomack all welcome visitors as you gradually make your way north east.

Tain Golf club, apart from offering a testing 6,000 yards (par 70) is the longest course in Ross-shire, is fully licensed and has full catering facilities and makes visitors and golf societies very welcome throughout the year. The highlight of the season is the Tain Golf Week (generally the first week in August) with a comprehensive programme of varied competitions running throughout and plenty of highland whisky as prizes if you are lucky enough to be on form. Full particulars of the 1994 programme obtainable from the secretary.

Before you "Turn the Corner" to Dornoch, Bonar Bridge offers a pleasant 9 holes (SSS 63) where visitors again are welcome all week, and then a string of courses (Golspie, Brora, Helmsdale, Lybster and finally Wick) await you on the last 40 mile stretch or so of this most pleasant coastline.

The "Top" of Scotland, while most famous for spectacular cliff and rock formations and abounding with walkers, climbers and fishermen, still has time to offer the golfer a testing course at Reay (near Thurso) and the Thurso Club itself nearby makes visitors welcome all year round. The town enjoys a deserved reputation for north of Scotland hospitality.

The majority of visitors to the north west corner of the country are not, in the main, considering golf. Should you be lucky enough to have the clubs in the boot, however, you can boast to your friends that you played on the most northerly course on the Scottish mainland if you enjoy the 9 holes at Durness; 5,500 yards or thereby laid out along the clifftops on this most beautiful part of Scotland and if nothing else you will enjoy the wonderful bird-life along the cliffs and coastline.

The Orkney and Shetland Islands, despite their remoteness, cater well for golfers and the Kirkwall course, above lovely Kirkwall Bay in Orkney, Stromness and Westray offer excellent sport and great hospitality (well I remember a weekend trip there many years ago when the golfing contest against the locals seemed of secondary importance to the entertainment in the clubhouse afterwards). The beautiful Shetland Islands, where you must not be without camera for sunrises, sunsets and glorious coastlines, provides golfing entertainment at Lerwick where the 18 hole Dale course (SSS 70) welcomes visitors all year round for very modest daily charges.

The breathtaking scenery of the north west mainland particularly the Lochinver, Scourie and Ullapool areas probably occupy most of the attention of visitors to this part of the world. Golf is not forgotten however, and the little 9-hole course at Lochcarron (only 1,733 yards) and the 9 holes at Gairloch offer you an opportunity to get the clubs out and enjoy both sport and scenery.

The Isle of Skye, famous for the cuillins, the little harbours, the roaring burns, the malt whisky, and perhaps less so, for golf, offers two 9-hole courses at Sconser (the Isle of Skye Club) and at Skeabost Bridge. The former, at just under 4,800 yards, has a standard scratch score of 63 while Skeabost has a real "fun" 9 holes with a standard scratch of 29. Once again, a lovely experience.

We must not forget that Mallaig, one of the main departure points on the mainland for a visit to Skye, provides golfing recreation at Traigh, while further inland, and to the southern part of the region, 9 holes at Fort Augustus at the southern end of Loch Ness and a testing 18 holes at Fort William also cater for the visiting golfer.

The Outer Hebrides, on the face of it, would probably be the last place you would anticipate finding golf. Not the case, however, with the links-land (Askernish) course on South Uist available, although by far the better known is the Stornoway club which is some half a mile from the town centre on the Ness Road. (I am indebted to club secretary Gordon Davies for a comprehensive description of the club and its facilities - I wish there was space to print all the details), suffice to say that Stornoway is now extended to 18 holes and plays harder than its 5,178 yards (SSS 66) would suggest. Spectacular views and not a few very difficult holes make the course a joy to members and visitors alike (the latter being very welcome every day apart from Sunday). The club is open during the winter as well, catering is available, and for the family there is a leisure centre with all the usual facilities and miles and miles of lovely beaches to explore - and try to make the Western Isles' Golf Week between the 9th and 16th July.

This is a region which is not, perhaps, highly regarded for wonderful golf opportunites but what it lacks here and there in the quality or testing golf course, is more than compensated by the most beautiful scenery anywhere in the United Kingdom.

PERTHSHIRE

ABERFELDY

For further details contact:
**Dunolly House, Aberfeldy PH15 2BL.
Kenmore Street,   Tel: (0887) 20298**

Situated in Aberfeldy Village with its well-served tea rooms, restaurants and hotels. Dunolly is within walking distance of Aberfeldy Golf Course and only 4 1/2 miles from the renowned Taymouth Castle Course. There are a further 5 courses within 15 miles and Gleneagles, Rosemount and St. Andrews are well within striking distance. Our B. & B. accommodation is top class from en suite at £18 to large and small rooms at £12. All rooms have colour TV and there are convenient games room, drying room and laundry room facilities. Aberfeldy Village's facilities are excellent.

THE GLENFARG HOTEL

★★

CARNOUSTIE · Ladybank · Crail · Scotscraig · ST. ANDREWS · Downfield · GLENEAGLES · Taymouth Castle · DALMAHOY · Lundin Links · ROSEMOUNT· Elie · Crieff

YOUR ONLY WORRY WILL BE CHOOSING WHERE TO PLAY ...

··· THE GOLFER'S HOTEL ···

Situated in the heart of Scotland's golfing country, yet only 35 minutes from Edinburgh and St. Andrews, this friendly and popular hotel is the perfect setting for your golf break.

With contacts at many clubs, we are happy to organise all your golfing requirements from giving first-hand advice on courses and green fees, to booking tee-times and refreshments. Our busy group package service includes discounted rates and a complimentary putter for the organiser.

Real ale bar · extensive bar menu · candlelit restaurant · bedrooms all ensuite · tea/coffee making · colour TV inc. Sky.

Write or phone for our informative golfing brochure which includes extensive information on courses, green fees and a range of packages. 2-day bargain breaks from £59.

**The Glenfarg Hotel, Glenfarg, Perthshire PH2 9NU.
Tel: 0577 830241.**

THE HOTEL COLL EARN

Auchterarder, Perthshire PH3 1DF

Coll Œarn House

A Victorian House privately owned, built 1870, restored to its old grandeur. Eight bedrooms all en-suite with colour TV, Direct Dial telephone, trouser press, tea/coffee making. Set in 6 acres of own grounds. Easily accessible from M90. **Prices £74 double/twin, £50 single. Special rates dinner, bed and breakfast £95 per double/twin, £62.50 per single.**

Tel: 0764 663553. Fax: 0764 662376.

Scottish Tourist Board
HIGHLY COMMENDED

Year after year our golfing guests return to Rosebank. They never tire of the many historic, scenic and championship courses surrounding Blairgowrie. Returning each evening, they appreciate fine food and the comfort expected of this Highly Recommended Georgian House. En-suite rooms, drying room, licensed, car park. Tee off times arranged. Special bargain breaks available January to October.

AA Highly Recommended:
RAC Highly Acclaimed.

P E R T H S H I R E

Rosebank House

Balmoral Road, Blairgowrie, Perthshire PH10 7AF.
Telephone: (0250) 872912

KINLOCH HOUSE HOTEL

With its oak-panelled hall and magnificent gallery Kinloch House is a fine example of a Scottish country house set in 20 acres of wooded policies and parkland, grazed by Highland cattle.

Situated 3 miles west of Blairgowrie, in the heart of beautiful Perthshire, Kinloch House offers the best of Scottish fare and a fine selection of wines and port.

An ideal golfing centre, 30 courses within an hour's drive. We should be happy to help plan your golf and book your tee off times.

By Blairgowrie PH10 6SG.
Tel: Essendy 0250 884 237
Fax: 0250 884 333

Please write or telephone for a brochure.
DAVID & SARAH SHENTALL

ANGUS HOTEL

46 Wellmeadow,
Blairgowrie.
Tel: (0250) 872455.

5 Day Golf Package Available
FROM £285.00
Includes Bed & Breakfast, Green Fees
for 5 Rounds of Golf
Including a St. Andrews or
Rosemount Course

Approximately 50 courses to choose from, all within 1 hour's leisurely driving. Blairgowrie provides an ideal base for your 1994 golfing holiday, coupled with our superb leisure facilities of indoor swimming pool, sauna, solarium, spa bath and squash courts.

We believe you will find our Packages hard to beat so contact us now for details.

AA **"ROCKDALE GUEST HOUSE"** RAC

BRITISH RELAIS ROUTIER
TASTE OF SCOTLAND RECOMMENDED
RESTRICTED HOTEL LICENCE

Accommodation consists of: 2 single rooms, 1 double room, 3 twin (1 en-suite–shower & toilet); 1 family room. All rooms have tea/coffee, central heating and fire certificate. TV lounge, separate dining room.

Bridge of Earn has the best of both worlds–country surroundings, but only 4 miles from Perth. It is an ideal centre for a golf break or touring. There are plenty of the well known courses and small scenic courses, all within a 30 mile radius. There is also fishing from the Earn or the Tay. We pride ourselves on our Scottish breakfasts and look forward to giving you some of the best home cooked dinners in the evening.

Prop: Anne Ewen, Rockdale Guest House, Dunning Street, Bridge of Earn PH2 9AA
Tel: (0738) 812281

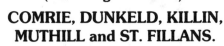

Balrobin Hotel

AA ★★ RAC

PITLOCHRY

Tel: (0796) 472901

Fax: (0796) 474200

Traditional Scottish country house. 16 ensuite bedrooms most with panoramic views. Residents only Bar (55 Malt Whiskey a speciality).

Golf breaks - in the heart of Scotland from £39 p.p.p.n. for D.B.B.

Also 2 bedroom luxury s/c apartment (sleeps 4).

CRAIGOWER HOTEL

Les Routiers

This privately owned hotel is situated in the centre of Scotland with many courses within easy reach. The hotel has 26 comfortable bedrooms, all ensuite, with hair dryers, TV, coffee/tea making facilities, telephone and offers freshly cooked food. There are two bars in the hotel, one of which is a friendly meeting place for locals. Pitlochry offers beautiful scenery with fishing, hill walking, theatre, golf and is central for many tours.

Small or large parties catered for.

Pets welcome.   *S.T.B. Commended*

Proprietors: J.C. & R.F. Wilson

Craigower Hotel, Atholl Road, Pitlochry PH16 5AB.

Tel: (0796) 472590

Queens Head Hotel

S.T.B. 3 Crown Commended

The Queens Head Hotel is the true sports enthusiasts ideal haven and golfers of all ages will find it the perfect base for 3 or 5 days golf where tickets at local clubs are easily obtained for as little as £60 for 5 days or £40 for 3 days. Also sample our excellent food. Everything homemade with local produce a must. Book now and make 1994 a Golfing Classic.   *Please ask for further details.*

Queens Head Hotel, Bridge Street, Kelso TD5 7JD
Tel: Kelso 224636. Fax: Kelso 224459.

A choice of 14 courses before dinner — Tasty 4 courses for dinner!

On our 2, 3 or 5 night breaks you can try a fresh course everyday. Afterwards you can enjoy a first rate dinner with our complimentary ½ bottle of wine.

At our friendly, family run hotel we make you genuinely welcome.

Please ask for further details:
36 The Square, Kelso
Roxburghshire TD5 7HL
Tel: 0573 223303   *AA ★★★*
Fax: 0573 225792   *RAC ★★★*

TELEPHONE DIALLING CODES

Many telephone dialling codes have changed this year. If you experience difficulty in connecting a call, please call Directory Enquiries–**192**–where someone will issue the correct number.

Please note: a charge will be placed for this service when using a private telephone.

DORNOCH CASTLE

Member of Scotland's Commended Hotels

This former bishop's palace, dating in part from 1550 is centrally yet peacefully located in the heart of Dornoch.
Most rooms look out over the lovely sheltered garden and Dornoch Firth; beaches and golf courses are within walking distance.
Superb food and outstanding wine list will make your stay here a truly memorable one.

Propr. M. Ketchin
Castle Street, Dornoch, Sutherland.
Tel: (0862) 810216. Fax: (0862) 810981.

SUTHERLAND

PARKHILL HOTEL

DURNESS
BY LAIRG
SUTHERLAND

Tel:
(097 181) 209/280

A small family run Temperance Hotel which takes pride in its Traditional Scottish Home Cooking

Central heating : Comfortable bedrooms

Ideal touring centre for birdwatching - beautiful sandy beaches, hill walking & dramatic scenery

Fishing by arrangement.
Close to scenic golf course

SPLENDID FAMILY HOLIDAY SPOT

Packed lunches available

PLEASE TURN TO PAGE 93 FOR LISTS OF GOLF COURSES

CORSEMALZIE HOUSE HOTEL

AA/RAC ★★★ S.T.B. 4 Crowns Commended

Peacefully situated country house hotel whose fifteen bedrooms are en suite, with radio, colour TV, direct dial telephone, tea/coffee making facilities and intercom. Ideal centre for fishing, shooting, riding, walking and golf with thirteen courses, to suit every standard of ability, in near vicinity. Golfing arrangemed on two local courses. Open from early March to mid-January (exc. Xmas Day & Boxing Day).

Port William Newton Stewart DG8 9RL.
Tel: Mochrum (098 886) 254.

Egon Ronay Recommended

WIGTOWNSHIRE

THE BEST 18 HOLES IN SCOTLAND?

One of the most pleasurable aspects of putting together this editorial on Golf in Scotland has been digesting the replies from golf club secretaries around the country to whom I had written asking for information on their clubs. Having asked each to pinpoint the hardest hole on their course - a subjective, but most thought-provoking request - there was no shortage of reading material when the replies came in and many are listed after their own regional editorials.

However, an idea had germinated. Would it not be fascinating to compile an imaginary Scottish course, which would consist of expert opinions on the hardest 18 holes in the country? - it did not take long to bring the idea to fruition.

Kind enough to answer by call - no doubt creating a lot of arguments among Scottish club golfers and visitors alike - and brave enough to put their heads on the chopping block were:-

Bernard Gallacher: - Captain of the Great Britain and European Ryder Cup Team; Professional at Wentworth; a Scotsman who has never forgotten his roots and whose golf began in Bathgate; one of the nicest men in British golf (although for the purpose of this exercise, I have ignored his leaning towards Hibernian F.C.)

David Huish:- Club Professional at North Berwick West Links; Scottish Professional Champion in 1975 and a member of the P.G.A. Cup Team; one of the most respected and popular professionals on the Scottish circuit over the last 20 years or so.

Jim Farmer:- A former footballing colleague of mine at Tynecastle (until a horrid knee injury forced his premature retiral); now back in his beloved St. Andrews with a superb golfing outlet; British Club Professional Champion in 1983;

regularly finishing in the top four or five on the "Tartan Tour" and a first class coach.

John Chillas:- Kind enough to take a little more time after penning his article (see elsewhere in the editorial).

The four did not collude - no contact was made with each other; I told none of them what the others had selected and the end result is fascinating! Here is their idea of "Scotland's Best 18 Holes"

1st hole, St. Andrews, Par 4, Bernard Gallacher:

"There cannot be another first tee in Britain which has the adrenalin pumping as fast as the first tee at St. Andrews on the first morning of the Open. If that wasn't enough to terrify the living daylights out of you, a fairly straight-forward drive then requires a very accurately judged second to clear the Swilcan Burn in front of the green. A wonderful start to your round."

2nd hole, Carnoustie, Par 4, Jim Farmer:

"So early in the round, this par 4 is very demanding. Normally into a cross-wind, driving past a bunker in the centre of the fairway is very difficult. Three further bunkers to the right and one to the left also jeopardise your chance of hitting the fairway. A very long second shot to a "valley" green (dunes on both sides) plus bunkers makes it hard to get close. Out-of-bounds at the back is the last straw.

3rd hole, Muirfield, Par 4, David Huish:

"A very accurate tee shot required here to hit the left centre of the fairway. Only thus will you get a clear view of the pin position for your second shot. If you haven't set up the drive properly, it is extremely difficult to get par."

4th hole, Turnberry, Par 3, John Chillas:

"The first short hole on the championship Ailsa Course - danger lurks around the corner. A mid-iron to an elevated green guarded by slopes to the front, left and back. The right side is not the place to go either. A good hole demanding a good shot."

5th hole, Glencorse, Par 3, Jim Farmer:
"Try this for a par 3. An elevated tee looks down into a perfect amphitheatre of a golf hole. Large mature hardwood trees protect the entire length. A burn in front of the green requires a 200 yard carry. It also protects the left hand side of the green and even if you do make the undulations of the green, regulation two putts are still difficult to achieve - a superb golf hole."

6th hole, Carnoustie, Par 5, David Huish:
"This is a real snorter of a hole and a perfect example of "risk and reward". The drive has to be aimed left of the bunkers to make the second shot easier - but watch out-of-bounds all the way down the left. (To take the right hand lie off the tee leaves a much more difficult second shot). The narrowing fairway means the second shot has also to be accurate, failing which the approach to a well guarded green is that bit harder. Very long, invariably into the wind, and a six would not be a disaster!"

7th Hole, Carnoustie, Par 4, John Chillas:
"Coming off the green of the huge 6th and finding, again, that you must play into the teeth of the inevitable west wind, with out-of-bounds all the way up the left, a bunker to guard the right hand side - what a way to enjoy yourself. A brave tee shot is required to set up the second to a well-guarded green. The problems do not end there - most putts have very large swings."

8th hole, Royal Troon, Par 3, Bernard Gallacher:
"Probably the most famous par 3 in Scotland - "The Postage Stamp" - is a gem of a short hole. Nothing but good old fashioned humps, hollows, whin and long grass to a marvellously constructed and protected green which always puts pressure on you in

trying to get down in two putts, even though the drive is accurate. I still don't know how Gene Sarazen got his Hole-in-One."

9th hole, Carnoustie, Par 4, Jim Farmer:
"If you need a four to protect your outward score, don't play this hole! Out-of-bounds all the way up the left (again) with bunkers an additional hazard. Four bunkers towards the right allow a width of only 20 paces to hit; go further right to avoid all these hazards? the ditch awaits you. You'll need a long iron or a wood for your second to a long narrow green guarded by bunkers."

10th hole, Royal Dornoch, Par 3, David Huish:
"This is only a short-iron shot but it is absolutely vital that you hit this green. There is trouble all over the place for a wayward tee shot and once again we have a hole where the shot from the tee makes or breaks the score. A cracking little par 3."

11th hole, Royal Troon, Par 4, John Chillas:
"A long par 4 demanding an accurate drive between the seas of whin bushes; the drive safely negotiated, you turn half-right. The second shot needs a fairway wood or long iron to the green, set left of the railway. Bunkered to the left, the "Chicken Line" is no guarantee of even a bogey five. You must attack this hole to get the reward of a par."

12th hole, Nairn West, Par 4, Jim Farmer:
"This is a very difficult drive with whins on both sides; also well placed bunkers which have to be eluded. The small plateau green has bunkers on both sides if you under-hit; an extremely hard par 4 for the professional, never mind the amateur."

13th hole, North Berwick West, Par 4, David Huish:
"This is a unique short par 4, where once again the tee shot requires to be close to the wall to allow your second shot to the green to give you the opportunity of two putts for

a par 4. The usual North Berwick wind blowing off the sea doesn't help either."

14th hole, Gleneagles, Par 4, John Chillas:
"A short driveable par 4 through a well-bunkered saddle to a huge green set in a hollow; bunkered very well right but, especially, left. A thrilling hole to play well when the tee shot hits the green and sets up a possible eagle."

15th hole, Newmachar, Par 3, Jim Farmer:
"This is a great short hole where you can require a driver into the east wind - normally a three iron, on the prevailing westerlies is the club. A large deep bunker protects the left hand side of the green which lies at an angle to the tee; two large swales don't make it any easier to get near the flag and possibly produce a birdie chance."

16th hole, Turnberry, Par 4, David Huish:
"An extremely difficult par 4 irrespective of the direction from which the Turnberry wind blows; the bunker in front of the green awaits any mis-hit or clubbing error and you can be well satisfied if you leave this green with your par."

17th hole, Muirfield, Par 5, Bernard Gallacher:
"I didn't choose this hole just because Lee Trevino killed off Tony Jacklin with that cruel chip all those years ago! A wonderful golf hole which puts you under pressure so near the end of a round - particularly if you're in a potentially winning position (ask Paul Azinger). Often sets up victory at the 18th, but also creates thoughts of suicide if things go badly wrong - which they often do on this hole."

18th hole, Carnoustie, Par 4, Bernard Gallacher:
"Arguably the finest finishing hole anywhere in Britain. Two jousts with the Barry Burn required, the first off the tee and any element of "hook" will find you in water (or

at the top end of the town council's putting green). Depending on the tee shot position, you have to decide whether to carry the second stretch of the burn (some 10 or 12 yards wide in front of the green) or lay up and hope that you can get up and down for your par. The brave go for the green and hope to miss the bunkers which protect it right and left. A fantastic finish and a near impossible par if the wind is off the east."

It would be lovely to see if any of our professionals could produce a score of 69 on that lot. And the selection of five holes at Carnoustie needs no further comment from me. Picturing the selections in the mind's eye and trying to imagine how I would cope with them (never mind the professionals), in a tournament-type atmosphere is quite frightening. I hope if nothing else, it stimulates a bit of interest and discussion around the club houses in 1994.

Editor's footnote: Jim Farmer found the above exercise so difficult and got so frustrated that he included four further holes on his list. I make no apology for adding them on and thank Jim for the extra time which he took - it simply proves what a host of fantastic possiblities exist in looking at the courses around the country. Here are Jim's further choices and comments:

1st hole, Muirfield - Par 4 (447 yards)
"As we only get to play this course in major championships, the rough on each side of the fairway makes this hole, as it is relatively flat with two fairway bunkers to catch the extra powered hook. Bearing in mind that this is your opening hole and that you are hitting into the prevailing wind, finishing on the fairway of this dog-leg is no easy task. A good drive will leave you with a long iron or even a second wood to a reasonably fair green, but you must beware of the bunker waiting to grab your ball if you dare cut or

pull. A five will be acceptable at this hole but a nice four makes you feel like you've secured a birdie. It is not difficult to take six; eight out of ten for difficulty."

4th hole, Gleneagles (Kings Course), Par 4 (466 yards)

"Standing on the tee you could be forgiven for thinking this hole was a par 5. You must hit a solid drive up the left centre, which is the only semi-flat part of a very narrow fairway. You are then left with 200 yards plus, uphill to a very narrow entrance protected by a large bunker on the right with a 15 foot drop on the left. The safe route is towards the back "fatter" part of the green, but even then having arrived safely, you're not finished. Try not to three putt this very difficult green. Treat a five here as a par, and if you are fortunate enough to take four then it feels like a birdie; smile sweetly and count your blessings because trying to play this hole as a three shot par 5 is still extremely difficult with such a small landing area for the second shot. 10 out of 10 for difficulty."

14th hole, Clydebank Municipal (Dalmuir), Par 3 (240 yards)

"This hole is called "Gully" but personally I would call it "help". The length of the hole itself produces its obvious problems but when you position a 30 foot gorge full of mature trees, shrubs and a burn between tee and green, stretching for almost the entire length of the hole, yet another dimension is added. Add to this a fall to the left which takes you down to the third tee, 70 yards from the green and 30 feet beneath it and you will understand why you must not hook off the tee. If you go right there are more 30 foot trees and shrubs so it is not advisable to "let one go" on the prevailing westerlies. I have used a driver everytime I have played this hole but trying to hit the tiny green is not my idea of fun. A great hole for the

solid striker but many an amateur will ruin an otherwise good score card at this hole. 10 out of 10 for difficulty (again, the hardest golf hole I have ever played, without a doubt."

17th hole, St. Andrews (Old Course) - Par 4 (461 yards)

"The famous "Road Hole" coming so late in the round, as you step on the tee, it's a case of "please, please - let me make 4."

Depending on the wind, a solid drive drawing off the Old Course Hotel makes life much easier. Straight over the old coal sheds takes you safely into the middle of the fairway; block the drive and it will cost you dear to get your ball back from an Old Course Hotel bedroom; hook the drive and a five or a six will inevitably result. Having survived the tee shot, the dilemma continues when you see the plateau green sitting at what appears to be the wrong angle to the fairway. The sands of Nakajema menacingly await the smallest of pulls or even a wayward chip or putt. Go right and the tarmac awaits you - a wall beyond, with out-of-bounds, possibly for the second time on this hole. If you are still reading (and playing) at this point then you can avoid the trouble with your second shot (which might range from a 3 wood to a mid-iron) by lagging the shot to a position short of all the hazards and then attempt a tricky pitch and putt or a Texas Wedge.

Four at the road hole is memorable, five is a good result and a six is not a disaster - it's as tough as that."

(Sincere thanks to Jim for these additional comments - he added, as a warning, that if the holes which he had chosen, together with others which he suspects his professional colleagues might select, were all strung together on one golf course, he would "give up golf tomorrow". I believe that says it all.)

DOUGIE DONNELLY

E ven among golf fanatics I like to think that I am a member of a relatively small group of nutcases! Many times in my life my day has ended at 3.50am. Only once has it begun at that particularly ridiculous early hour - and golf was the cause of it.

Just a few days after the summer solstice, when the daylight hours are longest, a group of us (broadcasters, entertainers and former international football stars) set out to play 100 holes of golf in a single day.

99 of those holes were to be played on the lovely Isle of Arran in the Firth of Clyde, off Scotland's West Coast, with the century to be completed after a short helicopter flight to the mainland where an accommodating par 3 awaited - over water naturally - at the Gleddoch Hotel & Country Club, where later we would rest our aching limbs.

It was virtually certain that our limbs would ache, for each of us had to walk every step of the way. No buggies were allowed although volunteer caddies awaited our

arrival at each of the Island's seven courses. Our golfing marathon attempt had attracted a great deal of interest locally, because each of us had been sponsored to raise funds to benefit disadvantaged and handicapped children through the Scottish Committee of the Variety Club of Great Britain.

So the great adventure began, appropriately, at a unique golf course. Shiskine Golf Club at Blackwaterfoot is Britain's only 12 hole golf course and a fascinating test it is at any time of the day; at precisely 4am, as dawn broke over the Arran Hills, however, it is eerily beautiful. Hitting the first drive on the longest golfing day of my life was an exhilerating experience particularly as it was struck into the half-light of early morning.

Our group of three completed Shiskine's world famous twelve in little over an hour. The nine undemanding holes at Machrie Bay, 10 minutes up the coast, took us only 50 minutes - early morning golf has its advantages.

Lochranza in the far north of Arran has recently expanded to 18 holes from the original 9. The terrain is understandably a little rough but we scampered home in excellent time and allowed ourselves 20 minutes for a splendid cooked Scottish breakfast (bread baked on the premises) and reflected that we had completed 39 holes in less than 6 hours. (Sad to say, I have reported on major European tour events where some of the world's best players have taken nearly as long to play 18).

From Lochranza our mini bus delivered us to the wonderfully picturesque 9 hole layout at Corrie. It was a joy to play. Encouraged by the enthusiastic support of the local members, we were round in an hour or so and heading for the main population centre of the Island and our final three courses.

Whiting Bay is arguably the best course on Arran after Shiskine, offering superb views from its position right at the top of the island but the panorama is hard-earned with a stiff climb up the opening three holes. For legs tiring after 48 previous holes, they offered the first real challenge of our attempted century but having taken our total to 66 after descending the 18th, things became progressively more difficult.

Ironically we were exactly two-thirds of the hundred completed when the weather, previously benign, decided to turn nasty. It began to rain - and heavily at that.

By the time we holed out at the challenging final hole on Lamlash (another excellent 18 holes, but hilly) the standard of golf had deteriorated noticably, all of our intrepid band were soaked to the skin and even conversation had become difficult.

Only 15 holes now remained to complete our 99 on Arran, and beginning at the 4th we set out around Brodick's mercifully flat layout which meandered pleasantly around the bay. We made it, encouraged over the final stretch by the clattering arrival of the

helicopters which would take us back to the mainland and the 100th hole.

The first 99 had taken 15 minutes short of 16 hours. Apart from that long-forgotten breakfast break it had been non-stop. Lunch had been a succession of chocolate bars; we kept telling ourselves it was to give ourselves a much needed energy boost.

Abandoning our clubs to the ever present back up team who would deliver them to the mainland, courtesy of the early morning ferry, we climbed into the choppers clutching only an 8 iron and a putter with which to do battle with the 7th at Gleddoch.

Our trio duly completed a century of golf holes with two pars and a rapturously-received birdie. The great adventure was over and as we shook hands we reflected on feelings which ranged through relief, exhileration and sheer exhaustion.

Just for the record, our trio, counting one net score per hole off full handicap, managed 249 stableford points. The winning group, with ex-footballers whose claims of dodgey knees had proved risible, managed a superb 270 - in other words more birdies than pars! But the most satisfactory aspect of an unforgettable day was that an astonishing £30,000 had been raised for the Variety Club and thus our warm glow of satisfaction was not due entirely to a long-awaited bath in the hotel.

Over the years I have been enormously fortunate in the sport I love. I have broadcast from many of the world's great championships - from St. Andrews to Augusta and from Royal Troon to Muirfield Village. I have played some of the world's great courses, so many of which can be found in my own small country; and I have met most of my golfing heros. Thus I have rich memories of the game of golf and the people who play it - but maybe the greatest now is of a summer day on Arran, and of 100 holes in a row.

A DIFFICULT CHOICE - THERE IS SO MUCH AVAILABLE!

(John Chillas, former Scottish Professional Champion, Captain of the Scottish P.G.A. and now professional at Glenbervie looks at golf in Scotland with a professional eye).

There is no doubt that Scotland, though such a small country, is in the eyes of the world, the mecca of golf for players of all nationalities. Tourists from all over the world flock here with the intention of playing on (and hopefully taming) some of the oldest and most famous courses in the world. After hundreds of years in golf, the Scottish golfing fraternity has come across enthusiasts from all walks of life and from virtually every country in the world.

So what can it be that attracts all these people to Scotland? The answer, quite simply, is that Scotland is the home of golf. Many of our courses are steeped in history and tradition, from the early beginnings of the game in Musselburgh right through to the much-loved Open Championship Courses of Troon, Turnberry, St. Andrews and Muirfield.

The annual influx of tourists to Scotland (usually in July, around the time of the British Open) brings together golfers of all abilities, ages and personalities. One very pleasing aspect which is noticeable on the arrival of our foreign visitors is that the majority seem keen to involve other members of the family in a playing capacity if at all possible.

There can be few countries with the possible exception of the United States, which can offer so many courses in such close proximity to each other. Scotland offers endless possibilities for those who are planning long or short breaks and in some parts of the country it is possible with the

minimum of travelling time to play two or even three courses in one day. Many of these, it is true, lie in or around a major population centre such as Edinburgh, Glasgow or Aberdeen. Therefore there are many standards of accommodation available to suit your needs and the opportunity to play courses of very different characteristics in a short period of time certainly does not pose a problem. In the west of Scotland for example, after enjoying the fine parkland courses such as Haggs Castle and Whitecraigs, one can travel less than 30 minutes to one of the wind-swept Ayrshire links such as Royal Troon, Barassie or Glasgow Gailes. Such possibilities exist all over Scotland and even in the far north you would not be disappointed with courses of the calibre of Nairn, Lossiemouth and Royal Dornoch on offer.

On the same theme there is a superb range of courses within a very small area which, in my opinion, are a "must" for all visitors to Scotland. The Edinburgh and East Lothian area is one of the best, not just in Scotland but in the U.K. Edinburgh boasts a superb range of courses, from the exclusive clubs such as Royal Burgess and Bruntsfield right through to the Municipal courses at Braid Hills, which not only offer a stiff test of golf when the wind blows, but also unbeatable views of the city of Edinburgh.

The rolling parkland fairways of Duddingston, in the east end of the city, must also be a great attraction to the visiting golfer. This course, sited just below Arthurs's Seat, offers a stern but fair test for even the most accomplished golfer. The front nine, with several "gentle" par 5s, lulls one into a false sense of security. Once the golfer encounters the first few holes on the back nine, which require a variety of different shots to complete them successfully, the course really begins to show its teeth.

Moving out of Edinburgh and following the east coast the standard of courses becomes even higher. Ten minutes outside the city boundary one encounters courses of the standard of Longniddry, another fine 18 holes which offers a combination of parkland and links and a variation of long par 4s and testing par 3s which makes this a memorable golfing experience.

Just ten minutes down the coast, Gullane, a golfing haven, beckons with a reputation for lightning-fast greens and tremendous value for money. There are three courses at Gullane and the view of many of my fellow professionals is that No. 1 is an excellent rival to close-by Muirfield with many testing holes in both halves. No. 2 and No. 3 are both pleasant links courses with many fine holes but remember to take plenty balls with you as the rough at Gullane can be fearsome!

No doubt it will be the aim of every visitor to play Muirfield, which regretably is not always an easy task. This is widely regarded as one of the best and toughest courses in Britain - indeed it may even be such, especially if the wind blows, and the last nine holes must be some of the toughest on the Open Championship,rota. Remember, if you are lucky enough to play at Muirfield, to try Lee Trevino's magical pitch at the 17th which in 1972, many believe, ruined the remainder of Tony Jacklin's career as a top tournament professional.

Further exploration down the coast will be rewarded with the discovery of another well-known golfing town, North Berwick. On offer are two vastly different courses, one which lies on relatively flat links on the west side and the other known as "The Glen" which is undoubtedly one of the best kept municipal courses in Scotland.

The courses which I have described in the last few paragraphs (from Bruntsfield in the west to North Berwick in the east) are less than 40 mile apart and hence any combination can be comfortably negotiated in one day. There are few other parts of Scotland which are blessed with so many fine courses in such a small area (with the possible exception of the Ayrshire coast) and a carefully planned trip by any visitor to Scotland should provide a once-in-a-liftime experience. The weather may not be guaranteed but the welcome from the club professional, the standard of the courses and the hospitality of club stewards and members will, I am sure, be a delightful experience for all.

PLEASE TURN
TO PAGE 93
FOR LISTS OF
GOLF COURSES

ACKNOWLEDGEMENTS

Directly or indirectly, huge numbers of people have helped me and while some (perhaps "models" for a few of the shots) were fully aware of my purpose many others have been blissfully unaware of the contributions they have made - so they deserve to be first.

Greenkeepers and their staff around Scotland are justifiably proud of their courses and of the reputation that they have helped Scotland to maintain as the most beautifully varied and natural habitat for golf in the world. Enormous hours and very hard work are involved - and for the magnificence of the courses which I have been priviliged to photograph, I give them my sincere thanks (I hope I did not forget to replace any divots or put the bunker rakes back where I found them.)

Next, the club secretaries around the country who took time to reply to my questionnaire - it is obviously not possible to include every item of information received but it was all examined thoroughly and if it is not used this year, then I am sure it will be in years to come.

I would also thank club members, those who occasionally were guinea pigs and those perhaps who were a bit non-plussed at the sight of a "spy" in their midst. I hope I did not interfere with the enjoyment of their rounds - and I know, on at least one occasion, that a putt of approximately 25ft dropped as I took the shot!

Finally, to my celebrities: Bernard Gallacher, John Chillas, Jim Farmer, David Huish, and Dougie Donnelly for taking time amidst very busy schedules to produce excellent and thought-provoking contributions, and in Dougie Donnelly's case, final proof that golfers are idiots! Their experiences and "hands on" opinions on the Scottish golfing scene add the real element to my own modest efforts from a distance of about 3 games a year. I would like to bet that "the best 18 in Scotland" will cause a few arguments around club lounges before the winter is out.

Old Course at St. Andrews.

Aberdeen

Aberdeenshire

Balgownie Golf Course

Royal Aberdeen Golf Club (2 courses),
Balgownie, Bridge of Don.
Tel: (0224) 702571 (Club-house).
Balgownie Links - 18 holes, length of course 6372 yds.
Par 70
Silverburn Links - 18 holes, length of course 4066 yds.
Par 60
Charges: Balgownie - £28 per round, £35 daily. Silverburn - £14 per round, £17.50 daily.
For advance reservations Tel: (0224) 702221.
A practice area and full catering facilities.
Visitors welcome - weekend restrictions. Letter of introduction required.
Secretary: Mr. Fraser Webster - Tel: (0224) 702571.
Professional: Mr. Ronnie MacAskill - Tel: (0224) 702221.

*Balnagask Golf Club

Nigg Bay Golf Club
St Fittick's Road, Aberdeen.
Tel: (0224) 871286.
18 holes, length of course 5521 m/6042 yds.
SSS 69
Charges: £4.20 round.
A practice area is available.
Visitors are welcome all week.
Secretary: Harry Hendry · Tel: (0224) 871286.

*Bon Accord Municipal Golf Club

19 Golf Road, Aberdeen.
Tel: (0224) 633464.
18 holes, length of course 6384 yds.
SSS 70
Charges: Telephone Leisure & Recreation, (0224) 276276.
Visitors are welcome but must be accompanied by a member.
Secretary: John B. Miller - Tel: (0224) 633464.
Professional: Ian Smith - Tel: (0224) 641577.

Caledonian Golf Club

20 Golf Road, AB2 1QB.
Tel: (0224) 632443.
18 holes, length of course
6384 yds.
SSS 70
Charges: £4.80 (round).
For advance reservations Tel: (0224) 632269.
Caddy cars, practice area and catering facilities are available.
Visitors are welcome all week.
Secretary: John A. Bridgeford - Tel: (0224) 632443.

Deeside Golf Club

Bieldside AB1 9DL.
Tel: (0224) 869457.
18 holes, length of course 5972 yds.
SSS 69
Charges: £20 per day; £25 weekends & bank holidays.
A practice area, caddy cars and catering facilities are available.
Visitors are welcome Monday to Friday and Sunday.
Professional: Frank Coutts · Tel: (0224) 861041.

*Kings Links Golf Course

Contact Aberdeen District Council, Aberdeen Leisure, Contract Services Division, 38 Powis Terrace, Aberdeen AB9 2RF.
Tel: (0224) 480281.
18 holes, length of course 6384m/5835 yds.
SSS 70
Charges: £6 adults, £3 juniors per round.
For reservations Tel: (0224) 632269.
Professional: Mr. R. McDonald, Golf Shop, Golf Road, Aberdeen. Tel: (0224) 641577.

Murcar Golf Club

Bridge of Don,
Aberdeen AB2 8BD.
Tel: (0224) 704345.
18 holes, length of course 6240 yds.
SSS 70
Charges: £16 round, £20 daily.
For advance reservations Tel: (0224) 704354/704370.
Caddy cars and catering facilities are available.
Visitors are welcome all week except Saturdays, Sundays before Noon and Wednesday afternoons.
Secretary: R. Matthews - Tel: (0224) 704354.

Westhill Golf Club (1977)

Westhill Heights,
Westhill, Skene, Aberdeenshire.
Tel: (0224) 740159.
18 holes, length of course 5921 yds.
SSS 69
Charges: £10 round (Mon-Fri), £13 (Sun & Public Holidays), £13 day ticket, £16 (Sun & Public Holidays).
For advance reservations Tel: (0224) 740159.
Caddy cars, practice area and catering facilities are available.
Visitors are welcome all week except Saturdays and Mon-Fri 4.00-7.00pm.
Secretary: John L. Webster - Tel: (0224) 740957.
Professional: R. McDonald - Tel: (0224) 740159.

Aberdour

Fife

Aberdour Golf Club

Seaside Place, Aberdour,
Fife KY3 0TX.
Tel: (0383) 860688.
18 holes, length of course 5460 yds.
SSS 67
Charges: Mon-Fri £15 round, £22 per day ticket.
For advance reservations Tel: (0383) 860256.
Catering facilities are available.
Visitors are welcome all week.
Secretary: J.J. Train, Tel: (0383) 860080.
Professional: Gordon MacCallum
Tel: (0383) 860256.

Aberfeldy

Perthshire

Aberfeldy Golf Club

Taybridge Road, Aberfeldy.
Tel: (0887) 820535.
9 holes, length of course 5100m/5577 yds.
SSS 67
Charges: £14 daily, £40 weekly.
A practice area, caddy cars and catering facilities are available.
Secretary: A.M. Stewart Tel: (0887) 820117.
Advance bookings at weekends in June, July and August.

* MUNICIPAL COURSES

Please mention this Pastime Publications guide 93

Aberfoyle
Stirlingshire

Aberfoyle Golf Club
Braeval, Aberfoyle.
Tel: (Aberfoyle) 08772 493.
18 holes, length of course
4760m/5204 yds.
SSS 66
Charges: Round weekday £12,
£16 daily. Round weekend £16,
£24 daily.
For advance reservations Tel:
(08772) 493.
Visitors are welcome all week,
restrictions at weekends.
Secretary: R.D. Steele
Tel: Aberfoyle 638.

Aberlady
East Lothian

Luffness New Golf Club
The Clubhouse,
Aberlady, EH32 0QA.
Tel: (0620) 843336.
18 Holes, length of course
6122 yds.
SSS 69
Charges: On application.
For advance reservations Tel:
(0620) 843336.
A practice area and catering
facilities are available.
Visitors are welcome weekdays
only by introduction.
Secretary: Lt. Col. J.G. Tedford
Tel: (0620) 843336.
Clubmaster: Tel - (0620)
843376.

Aboyne
Aberdeenshire

Aboyne Golf Club
Formaston Park, Aboyne.
Tel: Aboyne 2328.
18 holes, length of course
5910 yds.
SSS 68
Charges: £17 daily, £13 round
(Mon-Fri), £20 daily (Sat/Sun).
For advance reservations Tel:
(03398) 86755 (Secretary).
A practice area, caddy cars and
catering facilities are available.
Visitors are welcome all week.
Secretary: Mrs. Mairi MacLean
Tel: (03398) 87078.
Professional: I. Wright.

Airdrie
Lanarkshire

Airdrie Golf Club
Glenmavis Road,
Airdrie ML6 0PQ.
Tel: Airdrie 62195.
(Further details on application)

Easter Moffat Golf Club
Mansion House, Plains.
Tel: Caldercruix 842878.
18 holes, length of course
5690m/6222 yds.
SSS 70
Charges: £12 round, £18 daily.
For advance reservations Tel:
Caldercruix 842878.
A practice area is available.
Visitors are welcome Monday
to Friday.
Secretary: Mr. J.G. Timmons
Tel: (0236) 761440 or 441330.
Professional: Mr. B. Dunbar.

Alexandria
Dunbartonshire

Vale of Leven Golf Club
Northfield Road, Bonhill.
Tel: Alexandria 52351.
18 holes, length of course
5165 yds.
SSS 66
Charges: Mon-Fri £10 per
round, £15 per day ticket.
Weekends: £12 per round, £20
per day ticket.
Catering facilities are available.
Visitors are welcome all week.
Discount for parties on
application to secretary.
Secretary: W. McKinlay
Tel: Alexandria 52508.

Alford
Aberdeenshire

Alford Golf Club,
Montgarrie Road,
Alford.
Tel: (09755) 62178.
18 holes, length of course
5290 yds.
SSS 66
Charges: Mon-Fri - £8,
Weekend - £12 per round. Mon-
Fri - £12, Weekend - £16 daily.
For advance reservations Tel:
(09755) 62178.
A practice area and catering
facilities are available.

Visitors are welcome all week.
Please check for weekends.
Secretary: Mrs. Margery J. Ball
Tel: (09755) 62843.

Alloa
Clackmannanshire

Alloa Golf Club
Schaw Park, Sauchie,
by Alloa.
Tel: (0259) 722745.
18 holes, length of course
6240 yds.
SSS 70
Charges: £12 round, £20 daily.
For advance bookings contact
the Secretary.
A practice area, caddy cars and
catering facilities are available.
Visitors are welcome all week
except weekends.
Secretary: A.M. Frame
Tel: (0259) 750100.
Professional: Bill Bennett
Tel: (0259) 724476.

Braehead Golf Club
Cambus, by Alloa FK10 2NT.
Tel: (0259) 722078.
18 holes, length of course
6041 yds.
SSS 69
Charges: £12 weekdays, £18
weekends per round. £18
weekdays, £24 weekends daily.
For advance reservations Tel:
(0259) 722078.
Caddy cars, practice area and
catering facilities are available.
Visitors are welcome all week -
advisable to telephone in
advance.
Secretary: Paul MacMichael
Tel: (0259) 722078.
Professional: Paul Brookes
Tel: (0259) 722078.

Alness
Ross-shire

Alness Golf Club
Ardross Road, Alness,
Ross & Cromarty.
Tel: (0349) 883877.
9 holes, length of course
4718 yds.
SSS 63
Par 66
Charges: £2.50 round/daily
weekdays, £3.50 round/daily
Sat-Sun. Juniors £1.25, O.A.P's
£1.25. Seniors £10, juniors £5

weekly.
For advance reservations Tel: (0349) 883877.
A practice area and catering facilities are available.
Visitors are welcome all week.
Secretary: J.G. Miller
Tel: (0349) 883877.

Alva
Clackmannanshire

Alva Golf Club
Beauclerc Street, Alva.
Tel: (0259) 60431.
9 holes.
Charges: On application.
A practice area and catering facilities are available.
Visitors are welcome all week.
Secretary: Mrs. Annette McGuire · Tel: (0259) 60455.

Alyth
Perthshire

The Alyth Golf Club
Pitcrocknie,
Alyth PH11 8JJ.
Tel: Alyth 2268.
18 holes, length of course 5689m/6226 yds.
SSS 70 (Boxes 68)
Charges: Weekdays £17 round, £22 daily. Weekends £22 round, £27 daily.
For advance reservations Tel: Alyth 2268.
A practice area, caddy cars and catering facilities are available.
Visitors are welcome all week.
Professional: Mr. Tom Melville
Tel: Alyth 2411.

Annan
Dumfriesshire

Powfoot Golf Club
Powfoot, Annan.
Tel: Cummertrees 227.
18 holes, length of course 5465m/5977 yds.
SSS 69
Charges: £15 per round. £16 per round on Sundays after 2.45pm.
For advance reservations Tel: (0461) 202866/7.
A practice area, caddy cars and catering facilities are available.
Visitors are welcome all week except Saturdays and before 2.45pm on Sundays.
Secretary: R.G. Anderson

Tel: (0461) 202866/7.
Professional: Gareth Dick
Tel: (04617) 327.

Anstruther
Fife

Anstruther Golf Club
Marsfield, Shore Road,
Anstruther.
Tel: Anstruther 310 956.
9 holes, length of course 4504m.
SSS 63
Charges: £10 weekdays, £14 Sat/Sun per round.
For advance reservations Tel: Anstruther 310956.
Catering facilities are available.
Visitors welcome.
Secretary: A.B. Cleary.

Arbroath
Angus

Arbroath Golf Course (Public)
Arbroath Artisan Golf Club (Playing over above)
Elliot, By Arbroath.
Tel: 0241 72069.
18 holes, length of course 6078 yds.
SSS 69
Charges: £10 round (Mon-Fri), £15 round (Sat/Sun), £16 daily (Mon-Fri), £24 daily (Sat/Sun).
For advance reservations Tel: (0241) 75837.
A practice area, caddy cars and catering facilities are available.
Visitors are welcome all week.
Clubhouse facilities are not available on Thursdays.
Secretary:
John H.S. Lach-Szyrma
Tel: (0241) 73853.
Professional: J. Lindsay Ewart ·
Tel: (0241) 75837.

Letham Grange Golf Club
Colliston,
by Arbroath DD11 4RL
Tel: (024 189) 373.
Old Course - 18 holes, length of course Blue · 6954 yds: White · 6614 yds: Yellow · 6348 yds:
Red - 5780 yds.
SSS 72
Charges: £20 round, £30 daily (Mon-Fri); £25 round (Sat/Sun and public holidays).
New Course - 18 holes, length of course White - 5528 yds:

Yellow - 5276 yds: Red 4687 yds.
SSS 68
Charges: £12 per round, £18 daily (Mon-Fri); £15 round (Sat/Sun and public holidays).
1 round on each course - £26 weekdays; £35 weekends. (1993 charges)
A practice area, powered buggies and catering facilities are available.
Visitors are welcome all week.
Secretary: Pamela A. Ogilvie ·
Tel: (024 189) 373.
Professional: David Scott
Tel: (024 189) 377.

Arisaig
Inverness-shire

Traigh Golf Course
Traigh, Arisaig.
Tel: (06875) 645.
9 holes, length of course 2,400 yds.
SSS 66
Charges: £8 daily. £30 weekly.
Visitors are welcome all week.
Manager: Bill Henderson
Tel: (06875) 645.

Auchenblae
Kincardineshire

Auchenblae Golf Club
Auchenblae,
Laurencekirk AB30 1AA.
Tel: Laurencekirk 378869.
9 holes, length of course 2174 yds.
SSS 30
Charges: Season ticket restricted to those who had a season ticket in 1992.
Day ticket: Mon-Fri £6, Sat £7, Sun £8 - OAP's and juniors half price.
Visitors are welcome all week apart from Wednesday & Friday evenings (5.30 pm-9 pm).
Secretary: A.I. Robertson
Tel: Laurencekirk 378869.

Auchterarder
Perthshire

Auchterarder Golf Club
Orchil Road, Auchterarder.
Tel: (0764) 662804.
18 holes, length of course 5778 yds.

SSS 68
Charges: £13 round, £18 daily, weekdays. £19 round, £26 daily, weekends.
For advance reservations Tel: (0764) 662804/663711.
Professional shop and catering facilities are available.
Secretary: Mr. W.M. Campbell - Tel: (0764) 662804 (Office hrs. 9am-1pm).
Professional: Gavin Baxter Tel: (0764) 663711.

The Gleneagles Hotel Golf Courses
King's Course
The Gleneagles Hotel, Auchterarder PH3 1NF
Tel: (0764) 663543.
Telex: 76105
18 holes, length of course 6471 yds.
Par 70
Charges: On request.
Caddies, caddy car (on production of a medical certificate), practice area and catering facilities are available.
Golf available for residents and members only.
Golf Manager: Contact the golf office directly.
Professional: Ian Marchbank.

Queen's Course
Auchterarder, PH3 1NF.
Tel: (0764) 663543. Telex 76105.
18 holes, length of course 5965 yds.
Par 68
Charges: On request.
Caddies, caddy car (on production of a medical certificate), practice area and catering facilities are available.
Golf available for residents and members only.
Golf Manager: Contact the golf office directly.
Professional: Ian Marchbank.

The Wee Course
Auchterarder, PH3 1NF.
Tel: (0764) 663543. Telex 76105.
9 holes, length of course 1,481 yds.
Par 27
Charges: On request.
Practice area and catering facilities are available.
Golf available for residents and members only.

Golf Manager: Contact the golf office directly.
Professional: Ian Marchbank.

Ayr
Ayrshire

*Belleisle Golf Course
Doonfoot Road, Ayr.
Tel: (0292) 441258.
Fax: (0292) 442632.
18 holes, length of course 6088 yds (from yellow markers).
SSS 71
Charges: £15 round, £22 daily.
5-day ticket £60 (Mon-Fri only - 1 round of golf per day).
Weekly ticket £80.
For advance reservations Tel: (0292) 441258.
A practice area, caddy cars and catering facilities are available.
Visitors are welcome all week.
Professional: Mr. D. Gemmell Tel: (0292) 441314.

*Dalmilling Municipal Golf Club
Westwood Avenue, Ayr.
Tel: (0292) 263893.
18 holes, length of course 5724 yds.
SSS 68
Charges: £10 round, £18 daily.
Weekly £80 (1993).
For advance reservations Tel: (0292) 263893.
Caddy cars, practice area and catering facilities are available.
Visitors are welcome all week.
Secretary: Stewart D. Graham Tel: (0292) 262468.
Professional: Phil Chenney.

Ballater
Aberdeenshire

Ballater Golf Club
Victoria Road, Ballater.
Tel: (03397) 55567.
18 holes, length of course 5638 yds.
Par 67
Charges: On Application.
For advance reservations Tel: (03397) 55567/55658.
A practice area, caddy cars and catering facilities are available.
Visitors are welcome Monday to Friday.

Secretary: A. Ingram
Tel: (03397) 55567.
Professional: J. Blair
Tel: (03397) 55658.

Balmore
Stirlingshire

Balmore Golf Club
Balmore, Torrance.
Tel: (03602) 240.
18 holes, length of course 5615 yds.
SSS 67
Charges: £10 round, £12 daily, £60 weekly.
For advance reservations Tel: · 041 332 0392.
A practice area, caddy cars and catering facilities are available.
Visitors are welcome Monday - Friday with a member.
Secretary: G.P. Woolard
Tel: 041 332 0392.

Banchory
Kincardineshire

Banchory Golf Club
Kinneskie Road, Banchory.
Tel: Banchory 2365.
18 holes, length of course 5246 yds.
Charges: Mon-Fri £17.50 daily, Sat/Sun £19.50 daily.
For advance reservations Tel: Banchory 2447.
A practice area, caddy cars and catering facilities are available.
Golfing visitors are welcome.
Secretary: Mr. W.N. Donaldson
Tel: Banchory 2365.
Professional Mr. C. Dernie
Tel: Banchory 2447.

Banff
Banffshire

Duff House Royal Golf Club
The Barnyards,
Banff AB45 3SX.
Tel: (0261) 812062.
18 holes, length of course 6161 yds.
SSS 69
Charges: £11 (weekday) round, £15 (weekend) round, £16 (weekday) daily, £21 (weekend) daily.
For advance reservations Tel: (0261) 812062/812075.

A practice area, caddy cars and catering facilities are available. Visitors are welcome all week (but within restricted times, as shown on Tee Booking sheets. Handicap Certificate preferred).
Secretary: H. Liebnitz
Tel: (0261) 812062.
Professional: R.S. Strachan
Tel: (0261) 812075.

Barassie
Ayrshire

Kilmarnock (Barassie) Golf Club
29 Hillhouse Road,
Barassie, Troon KA10 6SY.
Tel: Troon 313920.
18 holes, length of course
5896m/6450 yds.
SSS 71
Charges: £35 daily (1992)
For advance reservations
Tel: Troon 313920.
A practice area, caddy cars and catering facilities are available.
Visitors are welcome
Mon/Tues/Thur/Fri.
Secretary: R.L. Bryce
Tel: Troon 313920.
Professional: W.R. Lockie
Tel: Troon 311322.

Barry
Angus

Panmure Golf Club
Burnside Road, Barry,
by Carnoustie DD7 7RT.
Tel: (0241) 53120.
18 holes, length of course
5761m/6302 yds.
SSS 70
Charges: On application.
For advance reservations
Tel: (0241) 53120.
A practice area, caddy cars and catering facilities (except Mondays) are available.
Visitors are welcome all week, except Saturdays.
Secretary:
Major (retd) G.W. Paton
Tel: (0241) 53120.
Professional: A. Cullen
Tel: (0241) 53120.

Bathgate
West Lothian

Bathgate Golf Course
Edinburgh Road,
Bathgate, EH48 1BA.
Tel: Bathgate 52232.
18 holes, length of course
6325 yds.
SSS 70
Charges: £20 daily (Mon-Fri),
£25 (Sat/Sun).
For advance reservations
Tel: Bathgate 630505.
A practice area, caddy cars and catering facilities are available.
Secretary: Mr. W. Gray
Tel: Bathgate 630505.
Professional: Sandy Strachan
Tel: Bathgate 630553.

Bearsden
Dunbartonshire

Bearsden Golf Club
Thorn Road,
Bearsden, Glasgow.
Tel: 041-942 2351.
9 holes, length of course
6014 yds.
SSS 69
Charges: On application.
Visitors are welcome, but must be introduced by a member.
Secretary: Mr.J.R. Mercer
Tel: 041-942 2351.

Douglas Park Golf Club
Hillfoot, Bearsden.
Tel: 041-942 2220.
18 holes, length of course
5444m/5957 yds.
SSS 69
Charges: £16 round, £22 daily.
For advance reservations
Tel: 041-942 2220.
Caddy cars and catering facilities are available.
Visiting parties by prior arrangement are welcome Wednesdays and Thursdays.
Secretary: D.N. Nicolson
Tel: 041-942 2220.
Professional: D. Scott
Tel: 041-942 1482.

Windyhill Golf Club
Windyhill, Bearsden G61 4QQ.
Tel: 041-942 2349.
18 holes, length of course
6254 yds.
SSS 70

Charges: £15 daily.
For advance reservations contact the Secretary by letter.
A practice area, caddy cars and catering facilities are available.
Visitors are welcome all week except Sat/Sun, by prior arrangement.
Secretary: Mr. A.J. Miller
Tel: 041-942 2349.
Professional: R. Collinson
Tel: 041-942 7157.

Beith
Ayrshire

Beith Golf Club
Threepwood Road,
Bigholm, Beith.
Tel: Beith 3166.
(Further details on application)

Biggar
Lanarkshire

Biggar Golf Club
The Park, Broughton Road,
Biggar ML12.
Tel: (0899) 20618.
18 holes, length of course
5416 yds.
SSS 66 Par 67
Charges: Weekday £5.50 per round, weekend £7.00, Jnrs & OAP's £3.50.
Daily £9.00 weekdays, £11.00 weekends, Jnrs & OAP's £5.50.
For advance reservations
Tel: (0899) 20319.
Caddy cars and catering facilities are available.
Visitors are welcome all week.
Secretary: W.S. Turnbull
Tel: (0899) 20566.

Leadhills Golf Course
Leadhills, Biggar,
Lanarkshire.
Tel: (0659) 74222.
9 holes, length of course 4150m.
SSS 62
Charges: Weekdays & weekends £4 daily/round.
Visitors are welcome all week.
Secretary: Mr. Harry Shaw ·
Tel: (0659) 74222.

Bishopton
Renfrewshire

Erskine Golf Club
(Further details on application)

Blackwaterfoot
Isle of Arran

Shiskine Golf and Tennis Club
Blackwaterfoot, Isle of Arran.
Tel: Shiskine 226.
12 holes, length of course
3000 yds.
SSS 42
Charges: £8 round, £10 daily
(Sept.-June). £8 round (July-
Aug.). Weekly £30.
Reduced fees for juniors.
(All charges inc. V.A.T.).
Eating facilities available (June
to September inc.).
Visitors are welcome.
Secretary: Mrs. F. Crawford
Tel: Shiskine 293.
Treasurer: E. Faulkner
Tel: Shiskine 392.

Blair Atholl
Perthshire

Blair Atholl Golf Course
Golf Course Road,
Blair Atholl.
Tel: (0796) 481407.
9 holes.
SSS 69
Charges: £8 round Mon-Fri; £9
round Sat/Sun. £36 weekly.
For advance reservations
Tel: (0796) 481407.
A practice area, caddy cars and
catering facilities are available.
Visitors are welcome all week.
Secretary: J. McGregor.

Blairgowrie
Perthshire

Blairgowrie Golf Club
Lansdowne Course,
Golf Course Road,
Rosemount PH10 6LG.
Tel: (0250) 872622.
18 holes, length of course
6895 yds.
SSS 73
Charges: On Application.
Caddies, caddy cars, practice
area and catering facilities are
available.
Visiting societies are welcome:

Mon, Tues & Thurs.
Secretary: J.N. Simpson
Tel: (0250) 872622.
Professional: Gordon Kinnoch
Tel: (0250) 873116.

Rosemount Course
Golf Course Road,
Rosemount,
Blairgowrie PH10 6LG.
Tel: (0250) 872622.
18 holes, length of course
6588 yds.
SSS 72
Charges: On Application.
For advance reservations
Tel: (0250) 872622.
Caddies, caddy cars, practice
area and catering facilities are
available.
Visiting societies are welcome
Mon, Tues, Thurs.
Secretary: J.N. Simpson
Tel: (0250) 872622.
Professional: Gordon Kinnoch
Tel: (0250) 873116.

Wee Course,
Golf Course Road, Rosemount,
Blairgowrie PH10 6LG.
Tel: (0250) 872622.
9 holes, length of course
4614 yds.
SSS 65
Charges: On Application.
Secretary: J.N. Simpson
Tel: (0250) 2622.
Professional: Gordon Kinnoch
Tel: (0250) 3116.

Blairmore
By Dunoon, Argyll

Blairmore & Strone Golf Club
High Road, Blairmore,
by Dunoon.
Tel: Kilmun 676.
9 (18) holes, length of course
1933m/2112 yds.
SSS 31 (62)
Charges: £8 daily Mon-Fri. £10
daily Sat/Sun. £30 weekly.
Visitors are welcome all week,
except Saturday afternoon.
Secretary: R.J.K. Dunlop
Tel: Kilmun 260

Boat of Garten
Inverness-shire

Boat of Garten Golf Club
Tel: 047-983-351.
Fax: 047-983-523.
18 holes, length of course
5837yds.
SSS 69
Charges: Mon-Fri £15 daily,
Sat/Sun £20 daily, £75 weekly.
For advance reservations
Tel: 047-983-282 (starting
sheet used everyday).
Caddies, caddy cars and
catering facilities are available.
Visitors are welcome.
Secretary: J.R. Ingram.

Bonar Bridge
Sutherland

Bonar Bridge · Ardgay Golf Club
Bonar Bridge.
9 holes, length of course
4626 yds.
SSS Men 63, Ladies 66.
Charges: £8 daily, £40 weekly.
For advance reservations
Tel: (08632) 750 (Groups only).
Visitors are welcome all week.
Secretaries: A. Turner
Tel: 054-982-248.
J. Reid - Tel: (08632) 750.

Bo'ness
West Lothian

West Lothian Golf Club
Airngath Hill, By Linlithgow.
Tel: Bo'ness 826030.
18 holes, length of course
6578 yds.
SSS 70
Charges: Midweek - £9 round,
£12 daily. Weekends - £14
round, £18 daily.
For advance reservations Tel:
Ian Taylor, Linlithgow 842286.
Caddy cars, practice area and
catering facilities are available.
Visitors are welcome mid-week
at all times. Weekend by
arrangement.
Secretary: T.B. Fraser
Tel: Bo'ness 825476.

Bonnybridge
Stirlingshire

Bonnybridge Golf Club
Larbert Road,
Bonnybridge FK4 1NY.
Tel: (0324) 812822.
9 holes, length of course
6058 yds.
SSS 69
Charges: £15 per round
weekdays, £25 per round
weekends. £25 daily.
Practice area and catering
facilities are available.
Visitors welcome by arrangement.
Secretary: C.M.D. Munn
Tel: (0324) 812822.

Bonnyrigg
Midlothian

Broomieknowe Golf Club
36 Golf Course Road,
Bonnyrigg EH19 2HZ.
Tel: 031-663 9317.
18 holes, length of course
5754 yds.
SSS 68
Charges: £15 round, £25 daily.
Sat/Sun £25 round.
For advance reservations
Tel: 031-663 9317.
A practice area, caddy cars and
catering facilities are available.
Visitors are welcome Monday
Friday.
Secretary: I.J. Nimmo
Tel:031-663 9317.
Professional: Mr. M. Patchett
Tel: 031-660 2035.

Bothwell
Lanarkshire

Bothwell Castle Golf Club
Blantyre Road,
Bothwell, Glasgow G71.
Tel: Bothwell 85 3177.
18 holes, length of course
5705m/6240 yds.
SSS 70
Charges: £14 round, £21 daily.
For advance reservations
Tel: Bothwell 85 2052.
A practice area, caddy cars and
catering facilities are available.
Visitors are welcome Monday ·
Friday.
Secretary: A.D.C. Watson ·
Tel: Bothwell 85 2395.
Professional: Mr. W. Walker ·
Tel: Bothwell 85 2052.

Braemar
Aberdeenshire

Braemar Golf Course
Cluniebank Road, Braemar.
Tel: (03397) 41618.
18 holes, length of course
4916 yds.
SSS 64
Charges: midweek £10 round,
£13 daily. Weekends £13 round,
£16 daily.
For advance reservations
Tel: (03397) 41618.
Caddy cars and catering
facilities are available.
Visitors are welcome all week.
Secretary: John Pennet
Tel: (0224) 704471.

Brechin
Angus

**Brechin Golf and Squash
Club**
Trinity,
by Brechin DDH 7PD.
Tel: (0356) 622383.
18 holes, length of course
5287 yds.
SSS 66
Charges: On application.
Catering facilities available.
Visitors are welcome without
reservation.
Secretary: A.B. May
Tel: (0356) 622326.
Professional: S. Crookston Tel:
(0356) 625270.

Bridge of Allan
Stirlingshire

Bridge of Allan Golf Club
Sunnylaw, Bridge of Allan,
Stirling.
Tel: Bridge of Allan 832332.
9 holes, length of course
4508m/4932 yds.
SSS 65
Charges: £7 round. £10 on
Sundays.
A practice area is available.
Visitors are welcome all week
except Saturday and during
Sunday competitions.
Secretary: A.M. Donoghue ·
Tel: Bridge of Allan 832007.

Bridge of Weir
Renfrewshire

**Ranfurly Castle Golf Club
Ltd**
Golf Road, Bridge of Weir.
Tel: Bridge of Weir 612609.
(Further details on application)

Brodick
Isle of Arran

Brodick Golf Club
Brodick, Isle of Arran.
Tel: (0770) 302349.
18 holes, length of course
4405 yds.
SSS 62
Charges: £8 round, £9 (Sat/
Sun). £11 daily, £12 (Sat/Sun).
Weekly £42.
For advance reservations
Tel: (0770) 302513.
A practice area, caddy cars and
catering facilities are available.
Visitors are welcome; parties by
advance reservation with
secretary.
Secretary: Mr. H.M. MacRae.
Professional: Mr. P.S. McCalla
Tel: (0770) 302513.

Machrie Bay Golf Club
Machrie Bay, by Brodick.
Tel: (0770) 850261.
9 holes, length of course
1957m/2143 yds.
SSS 61
Charges: £4 round/daily. £12
weekly.
Caddies, caddy cars and
catering facilities are available
Visitors are welcome all week,
except fixture days.
Secretary: A.M. Blair
Tel: (0770) 850 261.
Professional: W. Hagen
Tel: (0770) 850 261.

Brora
Sutherland

Brora Golf Club
Golf Road,
Brora KW9 6QS.
Tel: (0408) 621417.
18 holes, length of course
6110 yds.
SSS 69
Charges: £15 per day, £65 per
week.
For advance reservations
Tel: (0408) 621417.

Caddy cars, practice area and catering facilities (May-August) are available.
Visitors are welcome all week. Visitors can compete in any of our open competitions provided they have a current certificate of handicap with them.
Secretary: H. Baillie
Tel: (0408) 621417.

Buckie
Banffshire

Buckpool Golf Club
Barhill Road, Buckie.
Tel: (0542) 32236.
18 holes, length of course 6257 yds.
SSS 70
Charges: Per round - £10 Mon-Fri; £15 Sat/Sun. Daily tickets - £10 Mon-Fri; £15 Sat/Sun. £35 weekly (Mon-Fri).
Juniors under-16 receive 50% reduction.
For advance reservations Tel: (0542) 32236.
Catering facilities are available.
Visitors are welcome daily.
Visiting parties are welcome by prior arrangement.

Strathlene Golf Club
Tel: Buckie 31798.
(Further details on application).

Burntisland
Fife

Burntisland Golf House Club
Dodhead, Burntisland.
Tel: (0592) 874093.
18 holes, length of course 5391m/5897 yds.
SSS 69
Charges: £15 (weekday) round, £25 (Sat/Sun) round. £21 (weekday) daily, £35 (Sat/Sun) daily. Weekly by arrangement.
For advance reservations Tel: (0592) 873247/874093.
A practice area, caddy cars and catering facilities are available.
Visitors are welcome all week.
Secretary: I. McLean
Tel: (0592) 874093.
Professional:
Mr. Jacky Montgomery
Tel: (0502) 873247.

Caldwell
Renfrewshire

Caldwell Golf Club Ltd
Uplawmoor, Renfrewshire G78.
18 holes, length of course 6046 yds.
SSS 69
Charges £16 round, £24 daily.
For advance reservations Tel: (050 585) 616.
Caddy cars, practice area and catering facilities are available.
Vistors are welcome Mon to Fri.
Secretary: Ian F. Harper
Tel 0505-85-366.
Professional: Stephen Forbes
Tel 0505-85-616.

Callander
Perthshire

Callander Golf Club
Aveland Road,
Callander FK17 8EN.
Tel: (0877) 30090.
18 holes, length of course 5125 yds.
Charges: Weekdays £12, weekends £16 (round). Weekdays £17, weekends £21 (daily).
For advance reservations Tel: Society Bookings (0877) 30090.
Caddies, caddy cars, practice area and catering facilities are available.
Visitors welcome with Handicap Certificates or proof of recognised golf club on Wednesdays and Sundays.
Secretary: J. McClements
Tel: (0877) 30090.
Professional: W. Kelly
Tel: (0877) 30975.

Cambuslang
Glasgow

Cambuslang Golf Club
Westburn, Cambuslang.
Tel: 041-641 3130.
9 holes, length of course 6146 yds.
SSS 69
Visitors welcome when accompanied by member.
Secretary: William Lilly
Tel: 041-641 1498.

Campbeltown
Argyllshire

The Machrihanish Golf Club
Machrihanish, by Campbeltown.
Tel: Machrihanish 213.
18 and 9 holes, length of course 6228 yds.
SSS 70
Charges: Mon-Fri £15 (18), £5 (9) round. £20 (18), £8 (9) daily (Mon-Sun). Weekly £80 (18), £25 (9).
Children 14 years and under - half price on the 9 hole course.
For advance reservations Tel: Machrihanish 277.
A practice area, caddy cars and catering facilities are available.
Visitors are welcome all week.
Secretary: Mrs. A. Anderson ·
Tel: Machrihanish 213.
Professional: Mr. K. Campbell
Tel: Machrihanish 277.

Cardenden
Fife

Auchterderran Golf Club
Woodend Road, Cardenden.
Tel: Cardenden 721579.
9 holes, length of course 5250 yds.
SSS 66
Charges £6.60 daily, weekdays; £9.90 daily, weekends.
Visitors are welcome all week.
Secretary: Mr. Michael Doig
Tel: Cardenden 721877.

Carluke
Lanarkshire

Carluke Golf Club
Mauldslie Road, Hallcraig, Carluke ML8 5HG.
Tel: (0555) 771070.
18 holes, length of course 5308m/5805 yds.
SSS 68
Charges: £12 round, £18 day ticket.
For advance reservations Tel: (ProShop) (0555) 751053.
A practice area and catering facilities are available.
Visitors are welcome all week until 4pm, except Sat/Sun & Public Hols.

Secretary: J.H. Muir
Tel: (0555) 770620.
Professional: A. Brooks
Tel: (0555) 751053.

Carnoustie
Angus

Carnoustie Golf Links
Buddon Links Course
Links Parade,
Carnoustie DD7 7JE.
18 holes, length of course
5420 yds.
SSS 68
Charges: £8 round (1993).
For advance reservations
Tel: (0241) 53789.
Caddies, caddy cars and
catering facilities are available.
Visitors are welcome all week.
Secretary: Mr. E.J.C. Smith.

Carnoustie Golf Links
Burnside Course
Links Parade,
Carnoustie, DD7 7JB.
18 holes, length of course
6020 yds.
SSS 69
Charges: £13 round (1993).
For advance reservations
Tel: (0241) 53789.
Caddies, caddy cars (no caddy
cars Nov - Apr Incl.) and
catering facilities are available.
Visitors are welcome all week.
Secretary: Mr. E.J.C. Smith.

Caledonia Golf Club
Links Parade.
Tel: (0241) 52112.
(Further details on application).

Carnoustie Golf Club
3 Links Parade.
Tel: (0241) 52480.
Secretary: D.W. Curtis
Tel: (0241) 52480.

*Carnoustie Golf Links
Championship Course
Links Parade,
Carnoustie DD7 7JE.
18 holes, length of course
6936 yds.
Charges: £34 round. 3 Day ·
£102; 5-Day - £136 (1993).
For advance reservations
Tel: (0241) 53789.
Caddies, caddy cars (no caddy
cars Nov - Apr incl.) and
catering facilities are available.
Visitors are welcome all week,

except Saturday morning and
before 11.30 a.m. Sunday.
Secretary: Mr. E.J.C. Smith.

*Dalhousie Golf Club
Links Parade.
(Further details on application).

*Mercantile Golf Club
Links Parade.
Tel: (0241) 52525.
(Further details on application).

*New Taymouth Golf Club
Taymouth Street.
Tel: (0241) 52425.
(Further details on application).

Carnwath
Lanarkshire

Carnwath Golf Course
1 Main Street, Carnwath.
Tel: Carnwath 251.
(Further details on application).

Carradale
Argyll

Carradale Golf Course
Carradale, Kintyre.
Tel: (00833) 387.
9 holes, length of course
2387 yds.
SSS 63
Charges: £5 daily, £25 weekly.
For advance reservations
Tel: (05833) 387.
Visitors are welcome all week.
Secretary: Dr. J.A. Duncan
Tel: (05833) 387.

Carrbridge
Inverness-shire

*Carrbridge Golf Club
Carrbridge, Inverness-shire.
Tel: Carrbridge 623.
9 holes, length of course
5300 yds.
SSS 66
Charges: £8 Mon-Fri (except
July, Aug, Sept), £9 Mon-Fri
(July, Aug, Sept). £10 Sat/Sun
(1993).
For advance reservations
Tel: clubhouse 523.
Caddy cars, and light catering
facilities available.
Visitors welcome all week.
Secretary: Mrs. A.T. Baird
Tel: (047 984) 506.

Castle Douglas
Kirkcudbrightshire

Castle Douglas Golf Course
Abercromby Road,
Castle Douglas.
Tel: Castle Douglas 2801.
9 holes, length of course
5408 yds.
SSS 66
Charges: £10 round/daily.
Visitors are welcome without
reservation.
Secretary: A.D. Millar
Tel: (0556) 2099.

Clydebank
Dunbartonshire

Clydebank & District Golf Club
Glasgow Road,
Hardgate, Clydebank G81 5QY.
Tel: Duntocher 73289.
18 holes, length of course
5326m/5825 yds.
SSS 68
Charges: £12 round.
For advance reservations Tel:
Professional (Duntocher 78686).
A practice area and catering
facilities are available.
Visitors are welcome Monday
to Friday.
Secretary: W. Manson
Tel: Duntocher 72832.
Professional: David Pirie
Tel: Duntocher 78686.

Coatbridge
Lanarkshire

Coatbridge Golf Club
Townhead Road, Coatbridge.
Tel: Coatbridge 28975.
18 holes, length of course
5877 yds.
SSS 68
Charges: £1.75 round.
For advance reservations
Tel: Coatbridge 21492.
A practice area, caddy cars and
catering facilities are available.
Visitors are welcome at all
times, except 1st Saturday of
month.
Secretary: O. Dolan
Tel: Coatbridge 26811.

Drumpellier Golf Club

Drumpellier Avenue,
Coatbridge ML5 1RX.
Tel: (0236) 28723.
18 holes, length of course
6227 yds.
SSS 70
Charges: £18 round, £25 daily.
For advance reservations
Tel: (0236) 23065/28538.
A practice area, caddy cars and
catering facilities are available.
Visitors are welcome Mondays,
Tuesdays & Fridays.
Secretary: Mr. Wm. Brownlie
Tel: (0236) 23065.
Professional: Mr. K. Hutton
Tel: (0236) 32971.

Coldstream

Berwickshire

Hirsel Golf Club

Kelso Road, Coldstream.
Tel: (0890) 882678.
18 holes, length of course
6050 yds.
SSS 72 ladies
SSS 68 Men
Charges: Weekdays £10. Sat/
Sun & Public Hols. £15.
Caddy cars, practice area and
catering facilities are available.
Visitors are welcome without
reservation.
Secretary: John C. Balfour,
West Paddock, Duns Road,
Coldstream.
Tel: (0890) 883052.

Comrie

Perthshire

Comrie Golf Club

c/o Secretary,
10 Polinard, Comrie.
Tel: Comrie 670055.
9 holes, length of course
5962 yds.
SSS 69
Charges: £8 daily (£12
weekends
and bank holidays), £30 weekly.
For advance reservations
Tel: Comrie 670544.
A practice area, caddy cars and
catering facilities are available.
Visitors are welcome all week,
except Monday evenings from
4.30 pm.
Secretary: Mr. D.G. McGlashan.

Corrie

Isle of Arran

Corrie Golf Club

Sannox, Isle of Arran.
Tel: Corrie 223.
9 holes, length of course
1948 yds.
SSS 61
Charges: £6 round/daily. £25
weekly. £45 fortnightly.
Catering facilities are available
in the Summer only.
Visitors are welcome all week
except Saturdays.
Secretary: R. Stevenson.

Craignure

Isle of Mull

Craignure Golf Club

Scallastle,
Craignure, Isle of Mull.
Tel: (068 02) 351.
9 holes, length of course 2218m.
SSS 32
Charges: On application.
Visitors are welcome all week.
Secretary: Sheila M. Campbell
Tel: (068 02) 370.

Crail

Fife

Crail Golfing Society

Balcomie Club House,
Fifeness, Crail,
Fife KY10 3XN.
Tel: (0333) 50278.
18 holes, length of course
5720 yds.
SSS 68
Charges: £16 round, £24 daily,
weekday; £20 round, £30 daily,
weekend (1993).
Caddies, caddy cars, practice
area and catering facilities are
possible.
Visitors are welcome. Advanced
bookings for parties are
available.
Secretary: Mrs. C.W. Penhale
Tel: (0333) 50686.
Professional: G. Lennie
Tel: (0333) 50278 and
0333 50960.

Crieff

Perthshire

Crieff Golf Club Ltd

Perth Road, Crieff PH7 3LR.
Tel: (0764) 2397.

Ferntower Course:

18 holes, length of course
6402 yds.
SSS 71
Charges: On Application.

Dornock Course:

9 holes, length of course
2386 yds.
SSS 63
Charges: On Application.
For all reservations
Tel: (0764) 2909.
Buggies, caddy cars and
catering facilities are available.
Visitors are welcome all week
(it is advisable to book well in
advance).
Secretary: L.J. Rundle
Tel: (0764) 2397.
Professional: Mr. J. Stark
& D. Murchie
Tel: (0764) 2909.

Cruden Bay

Aberdeenshire

Cruden Bay Golf Club

Aulton Road, Cruden Bay.
Tel: (0779) 812285.
18 and 9 holes, length of course
5828 m/6370 yds.
SSS 71 (18), 62 (9)
Charges: £20 (18), £10 (9)
daily; £28 (18), £15 (9)
weekends daily. £85 weekly;
£140 fortnightly.
For advance reservations
Tel: (0779) 812285.
A practice area, caddy cars and
catering facilities are available.
Visitors are welcome all week
but restricted at weekends. No
society bookings at weekends.
Secretary: George Donald MBE
Tel: (0779) 812285.
Professional: Robbie Stewart
Tel: (0779) 812414.

Cullen
Banffshire

Cullen Golf Club
The Links, Cullen, Buckie.
Tel: Cullen 40685.
(Further details on application).

Cumbernauld
Dunbartonshire

*Palacerigg Golf Club
Palacerigg Country Park,
Cumbernauld G67.
Tel: (0236) 734969.
18 holes, length of course
5894m/6444 yds.
SSS 71
Charges: £7.50 round/daily.
For advance reservations
Tel: (0236) 721461.
A practice area and catering
facilities are available.
Visitors are welcome all week.
Secretary: David S.A. Cooper
Tel: (0236) 734969.

Westerwood Golf Club
Westerwood,
1 St. Andrews Drive,
Cumbernauld, Glasgow.
Tel: (0236) 725281.
18 holes, length of course
6139m/6721 yds.
SSS 72
Charges: On application.
For advance reservations
Tel: (0236) 725 281.
Caddy cars, practice area and
catering facilities are available.
Visitors are welcome all week.

Cupar
Fife

Cupar Golf Club,
Hilltarvit, Cupar.
Tel: (0334) 53549.
2 x 9 holes, length of course
5074 yds.
SSS 65
Par 68
Charges: £10 Mon-Fri. £12
Sunday.
Catering facilities are available.
Visitors are welcome all week.
Secretary: C. McCulloch
Tel: (0334) 52176.

Dalbeattie
Kirkcudbrightshire

Colvend Golf Club
Sandyhills, Colvend,
by Dalbeattie.
Tel: Rockcliffe (Kirkcudbright)
398.
9 holes, length of course
2322 yds.
SSS 63
Charges: £10 daily, juniors half
price, except Sat/Sun.
Catering facilities are available.
Visitors are welcome - (Apr-
Sept course closed: Tues. from
2pm, Thurs from 5.30pm.)
Secretary: Mr. J.B. Henderson,
9 Glenshalloch Road,
Dalbeattie. Tel - (0556) 610878.

Dalbeattie Golf Club
(Further details on application).

Dalkeith
Midlothian

Newbattle Golf Club Ltd
Abbey Road,
Dalkeith, Midlothian.
Tel: 031-663 2123.
18 holes, length of course
5498m/6012 yds.
SSS 69
Charges: £14 round, £20 daily.
For advance reservations
Tel: 031-660 1631.
A practice area, caddy cars and
catering facilities are available.
Visitors are welcome all week,
except Weekends and Public
holidays.
Secretary: Mr. H.G. Stanners
Tel: 031-663 1819.

Dalmahoy
Kirknewton EH27 8EB.

Dalmahoy Hotel, Golf
and Country Club.
Tel: 031-333 1845.
2 x 18 holes, length of courses
East 6097m/6664 yds, West
5317 yds.
SSS East 72, West 66.
Charges: £33 round East. £22
round West. £45 one round each
course.
Company/Society packages
available on request.
Visitors are welcome Monday-
Friday only (except residents).
Secretary: Jennifer Wilson.
Professional: Brian Anderson.

Dalmally
Argyll

Dalmally Golf Club
Dalmally, Argyll PA33 1AS.
9 holes.
SSS 62
Charges: £6 daily.
Visitors are welcome.
Secretary: A.J. Burke.
For Information
Tel: (083 82) 216/281/370.

Dollar
Clackmannanshire

Dollar Golf Course
Brewlands House,
Dollar FK14 7EA.
Tel: (0259) 742400.
18 holes, length of course
5144 yds.
SSS 66
Charges: £7 (Mon-Fri) round.
£11 (Mon-Fri) daily, £15 (Sat/
Sun) daily.
For advance reservations
Tel: (0259) 742400.
Catering facilities are available.
Visitors are welcome all week.
Secretary: Mr. J.C. Brown
Tel: (0259) 742400.

Dornoch
Sutherland

Royal Dornoch Golf Club
Golf Road, Dornoch.
Tel: (0862) 810 219.
18 holes, length of course
6017m/6581 yds.
Charges: On request.
For advance reservations
Tel: (0862) 810219.
Caddies, caddy cars, practice
area and catering facilities are
available.
Visitors are welcome all week.
Secretary: Ian C.R. Walker
Tel: (0862) 810219.
Professional: W.E. Skinner
Tel: (0862) 810902.

Drymen
Stirlingshire

Buchanan Castle Golf Club
Drymen.
Tel: (0360) 60369/07/30.
18 holes, length of course
6086 yds.
SSS 69

Charges: £20 round, £30 daily.
For advance reservations
Tel: (0360) 60307.
Visitors are welcome by
arrangement.
Secretary: R. Kinsella
Tel: (0360)60307.
Professional: Mr. C. Dernie
Tel: (0360) 60330.

Strathendrick Golf Club
Drymen.
9 holes, length of course 4962
yds (gents), 4518 yds (ladies).
SSS 65 (gents)
SSS 66 (ladies)
Charges: N/A.
Visitors accompanied by a
member are welcome all week,
restrictions on competition days.
Secretary: R.H. Smith
Tel: (0360) 40582.

Dufftown
Banffshire

Dufftown Golf Club
Methercluny, Tomintoul Road,
Dufftown.
Tel: (0340) 20325.
18 holes, length of course
5308 yds.
SSS 67
Charges: £7 (Mon-Fri), £8 (Sat/
Sun). £25 weekly.
Bar and catering available daily.
Visitors are welcome all week.
Secretary: Mr. A. Stuart
Tel: (0340) 20165.

Dullatur
Dunbartonshire.

Dullatur Golf Club
Tel: Cumbernauld 723230.
18 holes, length of course
6229 yds.
SSS 70
Charges: £18 daily; £10 (after
1.30pm).
For advance reservations
Tel: Cumbernauld 723230.
Caddy cars, practice area and
catering facilities are available.
Visitors are welcome Mon-Fri,
(except 1st Wed in month &
public holidays).
Secretary: W. Laing
Tel: Cumbernauld 723230.
Professional: D. Sinclair
Tel: Cumbernauld 723230.

Dumbarton
Dunbartonshire

Cardross Golf Club
Main Road, Cardross,
Dumbarton G82 5LB.
Tel: (0389) 841213.
18 holes, length of course
6469 yds.
SSS 71
Charges: £15 round, £25 day
ticket.
For advance reservations
Tel: (0389) 841350.
Caddy cars, practice area and
catering facilities are available.
Visitors welcome weekdays
only.
Secretary: R. Evans C.A.
Tel: (0389) 841754.
Professional: Robert Craig
Tel: (0389) 841350.

Dumbarton Golf Course
Broadmeadow, Dumbarton.
Tel: Dumbarton 32830.
(Further details on application).

Dumfries
Dumfriesshire

Crichton Royal Golf Club,
Bankend Road,
Dumfries DG1 4TH.
Tel: (0387) 41122.
9 holes, length of course
2,700 yds.
SSS 69 White
SSS 68 Blue
Charges: Weekdays £6,
Weekends £8 (9 hole).
Weekdays £12, Weekends £15
(18 hole). £35 Weekly.
For advance reservations
Tel: (0387) 41122.
A practice are and catering
facilities are available.
Visitors are welcome: Mon,
Wed, Fri, Sat & Sun.
Manager: Mr. R. Chapman
Tel: (0387) 41122.

Dumfries and County Golf
Club
Edinburgh Road,
Dumfries DG1 1JX.
Tel: (0387) 53585.
18 holes, length of course
5928 yds.
SSS 68
Charges: £21, (Sun £25) daily -
no round ticket. £70 weekly.
A practice area, caddy carts and
catering facilities are available.

Visitors are welcome all week,
except Saturdays.
Secretary: E.C. Pringle
Tel: (0387) 53585.
Professional: Mr. G. Gray
Tel: (0387) 68918.

Dunbar
East Lothian

Dunbar Golf Club
East Links, Dunbar EH42 1LP.
Tel: (0368) 62317.
18 holes, length of course
5874m/6426 yds.
SSS 71
Charges: Daily - £25 weekdays;
£40 weekends & Specified
holidays.
For advance reservations
Tel: (0368) 62317.
A practice area, caddies (if
reserved) and catering facilities
are available.
Visitors are welcome all week,
after 9.30 am (except Thurs).
Secretary: Mr. Don Thompson
Tel: (0368) 62317.
Professional: Mr. D. Small
Tel: (0368) 62086.

*Winterfield Golf Club
North Road, Dunbar.
Tel: (0368) 62280.
18 holes.
SSS 65
Charges: On Application.
For advance reservations
Tel: (0368) 63562.
Caddy cars and catering
facilities are available.
Secretary: Mr. M. O'Donnell
Tel: (0368) 62564.
Professional: Mr. K. Phillips
Tel: (0368) 63562.

Dunblane
Perthshire

Dunblane New Golf Club
Perth Road, Dunblane.
Tel: Dunblane 823711.
18 holes, length of course
5371m/5874 yds.
SSS 68
Charges: £15 round (Mon-Fri),
£22 (Sat/Sun), £22 daily.
(Charges subject to revision).
For advance reservations
Tel: Dunblane 823711.
A practice area, caddy cars and
catering facilities (by advance
order) are available.

Visitors are welcome Monday to Friday.
Secretary: R.S. MacRae
Tel: Falkirk 21263.
Professional: R.M. Jamieson
Tel: Dunblane 823711.

Dundee
Angus

*Camperdown Golf Course
Camperdown Park, Dundee.
Tel: (0382) 623398.
Visitors contact: Art & Recreation Division, Leisure Centre, Dundee
Tel: (0382) 23141 (ext. 413).
Secretary: K. McCreery
Tel: (0382) 642925.
(Further details on application).

Downfield Golf Club
Turnberry Avenue, Dundee.
Tel: (0382) 825595.
Fax: (0382) 813111.
18 holes, length of course 6804 yds.
SSS 73
Charges: £24 round, £36 daily (inc. weekends).
Caddies, caddy cars, practice area and catering facilities available.
Visitors are welcome weekdays and Sunday pm - parties welcome with pre-booking essential. Other times - Saturday and Sunday call starter on day of play after 8.00am.
Secretary: Brian F. Mole
Tel: (0382) 825595.
Professional/Starter: C. Waddell
Tel: (0382) 89246.

Dunfermline
Fife

Canmore Golf Club
Venturefair, Dunfermline.
Tel: Dunfermline 724969.
(Further details from the Secretary on Dunfermline 726098).

Dunfermline Golf Club
Pitfirrane Crossford, Dunfermline.
Tel: (0383) 723534.
18 holes, length of course 6237 yds.
SSS 70
Charges: £18 round, £25 daily.
For advance reservations

Tel: (0383) 723534.
Caddy cars, practice area and catering facilities are available.
Visitors are welcome Mon. to Fri.
Secretary: H. Matheson
Tel: (0383) 723534.

Pitreavie (Dunfermline) Golf Club
Queensferry Road, Dunfermline KY11 5PR.
Tel: (0383) 722591.
18 holes, length of course 5565m/6086 yds.
SSS 69
Charges: Weekdays £13 round, £18 daily. Weekends £24 daily, no round tickets. (1992).
For advance reservations - Casual visitors Tel: (0383) 723151, Parties, Societies etc.
Tel: (0383) 722591.
A practice area, caddy cars and catering facilities are available.
Visitors are welcome all week.
Secretary: Mr. D. Carter
Tel: (0383) 722591.
Professional: Mr. J. Forrester
Tel: (0383) 723151.

Dunkeld
Perthshire

Dunkeld & Birnam Golf Club
Fungarth, Dunkeld.
Tel: (0350) 727524.
9 holes, length of course 5264 yds.
SSS 66
Charges: On Application.
For advance reservations
Tel: (0350) 727564.
Caddy cars and catering facilities are available.
Visitors are welcome all week without reservation.
Secretary: Mrs. W.A. Sinclair
Tel: (0350) 727564.

Dunning
Perthshire

Dunning Golf Club
Rollo Park, Dunning.
Tel: 684747.
9 holes, length of course 4836 yds.
SSS 64
Charges: £7 round/daily, junior £3.50.

For Club/society bookings
Tel: (076484) 312 (Secretary).
Caddy cars available.
No visitors after 5pm Mon-Fri, unless accompanied by a member. No visitors before 5pm Saturday. No golf before 1pm on Sunday.
Secretary: Miss C. Westwood
Tel: (076484) 312.

Dunoon
Argyll

Cowal Golf Club
Ardenslate Road, Dunoon.
Tel: Dunoon 5673.
18 holes, length of course 5716m/6251 yds.
SSS 70
Charges: £13 round (Mon-Fri), £20 round (Sat/Sun).
For advance reservations
Tel: Dunoon 5673.
Caddy cars and catering facilities are available.
Secretary: Brian Chatham
Tel: Dunoon 5673.
Professional: R.D. Weir.

Duns
Berwickshire

Duns Golf Club
Hardens Road, Duns.
(Further details on application).

Durness
Sutherland

Durness Golf Club,
Durness, Sutherland.
9 holes, length of course 5545 yds/5040m.
SSS 68
Charges: £8 round/daily. £32 weekly.
For advance reservations
Tel: (0971) 511364 or 511351.
Caddy cars, practice area and catering facilities are available.
Visitors are welcome all week.
Secretary: Mrs. Lucy Mackay
Tel: (0971) 511364.

Eaglesham
Renfrewshire

Bonnyton Golf Club
Eaglesham, Glasgow G76 0QA.
Tel: (03553) 2781.
18 holes, length of course
6252 yds.
SSS 71
Charges: £25 daily.
Caddy cars, practice area and
catering facilities are available.
Visitors welcome Monday to
Friday.
Secretary: A. Hughes
Tel: (03553) 2781.
Professional: R. Crerar -
Tel: (03553) 2256.

East Kilbride
Lanarkshire

East Kilbride Golf Club
Nerston, East Kilbride,
Glasgow G74 4PF.
Tel: (00552) 20913.
18 holes, length of course
6384 yds.
SSS 71
Charges: £14 round, £20 daily.
Visitors welcome weekdays
only on application if members
of an official club. Weekends,
no visitors unless accompanied
by a member.
Secretary: W.G. Gray.
Professional: A.R. Taylor.

*Torrance House Golf Club
Strathaven Road,
East Kilbride G75 0QZ.
Tel: (03552) 49720.
18 holes, length of course
6415 yds.
SSS 71
Charges: £11.50 per round.
For advance reservations
Tel: (03552) 48638.
Caddy cars, practice area and
catering facilities are available.
Visitors are welcome all week
by arrangement with:
Recreation Manager (Golf),
Leisure Services Department,
East Kilbride District Council,
Civic Centre, East Kilbride.
Tel: (03552) 71296.
Professional: J. Dunlop
Tel: (03552) 71296.

Edinburgh

Baberton Golf Club
Baberton Avenue, Juniper
Green, Edinburgh EH14 5DU.
Tel: 031-453 3361.
18 holes, length of course
6098 yds.
SSS 69
Catering facilities available by
arrangement.
Secretary: E.W. Horberry
Tel: 031-453 4911.
Professional: K. Kelly
Tel: 031-453 3555.

*Braid Hills Golf Course
Braid Hills Approach,
Edinburgh EH10.
(Further details on application).

The Bruntsfield Links Golfing Society
32 Barnton Avenue, Davidsons
Mains, Edinburgh EH4 6JH.
Tel: 031-336 2006.
18 holes, length of course
6407 yds.
SSS 71
Charges: On Application.
For advance reservations
Tel: 031-336 1479.
Catering facilities are available.
Secretary: Lt. Col. M.B. Hext
Tel: 031-336 1479.
Professional: Brian MacKenzie
Tel: 031-336 4050.

*Carrick Knowe Golf Club
27 Glen Devon Park,
Edinburgh.
Tel: 031-337 2217.
(Further details on application).

*Craigentinny Golf Course
Craigentinny Avenue, Lochend,
Edinburgh.
Tel: 031-554 7501.
(Further details on application).

Craigmillar Park Golf Club
1 Observatory Road,
Edinburgh EH9 3HG.
Tel: 031-667 0047.
18 holes, length of course
5851 yds.
SSS 68
Charges: £12 round. £18 daily.
For advance reservations
Tel: 031-667 0047.
Caddy cars, practice area and
catering facilities are available.
Visitors are welcome on
weekdays before 3.30pm only

(not weekends).
Secretary: J. Brough
Tel: 031-667 0047.
Professional: B. McGhee
Tel: 031-667 0047.

Duddingston Golf Club
Duddingston Road West,
Edinburgh.
Tel: 031-661 7688.
18 holes, length of course
6078m/6647 yds.
SSS 72
Charges: Visitors (Mon-Fri) -
£20 round, £26 daily. Societies -
£17 round, £23 day (Tue &
Thurs only).
For advance reservations
Tel: 031-661 7688.
A practice area, caddy cars and
catering facilities are available.
Secretary: J.C. Small
Tel: 031-661 7688.
Professional: Mr. A. McLean.

Kingsknowe Golf Club Ltd
326 Lanark Road, Edinburgh
EH14 2JD.
Tel: 031-441 1145.
18 holes, length of course
5469m/5979 yds.
SSS 69
Charges £16 round, £20 daily
(weekdays), £25 round
(weekends).
For advance reservations
Tel: 031-441 4030.
A practice area, caddy cars and
catering facilities are available.
Visitors are welcome.
Secretary: R. Wallace
Tel: 031-441 1145.
Professional: A. Marshall
Tel: 031-441 4030.

Liberton Golf Club
297 Gilmerton Road,
Edinburgh EH16 5UJ.
Tel: 031-664 3009.
18 holes, length of course
5299 yds.
SSS 66
Charges: £15 per round, £25
daily.
For advance reservations
Tel: 031-664 1056
A practice area and catering
facilities are available.
Visitors are welcome all week -
Sat & Sun after 1.30pm only.
Secretary: A.J.R. Poole
Tel: 031-664 3009.
Professional: Iain Seath
Tel: 031-664 1056.

Lothianburn Golf Club
106a Biggar Road,
Edinburgh EH10 7DU.
Tel: 031-445 2206.
Visitors Welcome.
Secretary/Treasurer:
W.F.A. Jardine
Tel: 031-445 5067.
Professional: Paul Morton
Tel: 031-445 2288.
(Further details on application).

Merchants of Edinburgh Golf Club
10 Craighill Gardens,
Edinburgh EH10 5PY.
Tel: 031-447 1219.
18 holes, length of course
4889 yds.
SSS 64
Charges: £12 daily (no round ticket). Reductions for arranged parties.
For advance reservations
Tel: 031-447 1219.
Catering facilities are available by arrangement.
Visiting clubs welcome Monday to Friday by request to the Secretary.
Secretary: A.M. Montgomery
Tel: 031-447 7093.
Professional: Craig A. Imlah
Tel: 031-447 8709.

Mortonhall Golf Club
231 Braid Road, EH10 6PB.
Tel: 031-447 2411.
18 holes, length of course
5987m/6548 yds.
SSS 71
Charges: On application
Catering facilities available.
Visitors are welcome with introduction.
Secretary: Mr. P.T. Ricketts
Tel: 031-447 6974.
Professional: D. Horn.

Portobello Golf Club
Stanley Street, Edinburgh
EH15.
Tel: 031-669 4361.
9 holes, length of course
2167m/ 2400 yds.
SSS 32
Charges: Weekdays & Sat & Sun £3 (9).
For advance reservations
Tel: 031-669 4361.
Visitors are welcome all week.
Secretary: Mr. Alistair Cook.

Prestonfield Golf Club (Private)
6 Priestfield Road North,
Edinburgh.
Tel: 031-667 1273.
18 holes, length of course
5685m/6216 yds.
SSS 70
Charges: On application.
For advance reservations
Tel: 031-667 8597.
A practice area, caddy cars and catering facilities are available.
Secretary: M.D.A.G. Dillon
Professional: R. B. Commins

Ratho Park Golf Club
Ratho, Newbridge, Midlothian
EH28 8NX.
Tel: 031-333 1252.
18 holes, length of course
5398m/5900 yds.
SSS 68
Charges: £17.50 round, £27 daily, £30 weekend.
For advance reservations
Tel: 031-333 1406.
A practice area, caddy cars and catering facilities are available.
Visitors are welcome Tuesday, Wednesday and Thursday.
Secretary: Mr. J.C. McLafferty
Tel: 031-333 1252.
Professional: Mr. A. Pate
Tel: 031-333 1406.

Ravelston Golf Club
24 Ravelston Dykes Road, EH4
5NZ.
Tel: 031-315 2486.
9 holes, length of course
4754 m/5200 yds.
SSS 66 (men)
SSS 69 (ladies)
Charges: £12.50 round - visitors.
Visitors are welcome (Mon. to Fri.)
Secretary: Mr. Frank Philip.

The Royal Burgess Golfing Society of Edinburgh
181 Whitehouse Road,
Edinburgh EH4 6BY.
Tel: 031-339 2075.
18 holes, length of course
6494 yds.
SSS 71
Charges: On application.
For advance reservations
Tel: 031-339 2075.
Trolley and catering facilities are available.
Visitors/parties are welcome Mon-Fri.

Secretary: John P. Audis
Tel: 031-339 2075.
Professional: George Yuille
Tel: 031-339 6474.

*Silverknowes Golf Club (Private)
Silverknowes Parkway,
Edinburgh EH4 5ET.
Tel: 031-336 5359.
(Further details on application).

Swanston Golf Club
111 Swanston Road,
Edinburgh EH10 7DS.
Tel: 031-445 2239.
18 holes, length of course
5024 yds.
SSS 66
Charges: £10 per round. £15 daily.
For advance reservations
Tel: 031-445 4002 (Prof.)
Catering facilities are available.
Visitors are welcome 9am-4pm Mon-Fri.
Secretary: John Allan
Tel: 031-445 2239.
Professional: J. Scott-Maxwell
Tel: 031-445 4002.

Torphin Hill Golf Club
Torphin Road, Edinburgh
EH13 0PL.
Tel: 031-441 1100.
18 holes, length of course
4597m/5020 yds.
SSS 66
Charges: £10 weekdays, £16 weekends daily.
For advance reservations
Tel: 031-441 1100.
Practice area and catering facilities are available.
Visitors are welcome all week, except competition days (phone for details).
Secretary: R.A. Hawkes
Tel: 031-441 1100.

Turnhouse Golf Club Ltd.
154 Turnhouse Road,
Edinburgh.
Tel: 031-339 1014.
18 holes, length of course
6121 yds.
SSS 69
Charges: £14 per round, £20 daily.
For advance reservations
Tel: 031-539 5937.
Caddy cars, practice area and catering facilities are available.
Visitors are welcome (only as a

Please mention this Pastime Publications guide

society) Mon-Fri, except on competition days - usually Wednesday and Friday.
Secretary: A.B. Hay
Tel: 031-539 5937
Professional: J. Murray
Tel: 031-339 2201.

Edzell
Angus

The Edzell Golf Club
High Street, Edzell DD9 7TF.
Tel: (0356) 648235 (Clubhouse).
18 holes, length of course 6348 yds.
SSS 70
Charges: Weekday £17 round, weekend £22 round, weekday £25.50 daily, weekend £33 daily, £85 weekly.
For advance reservations
Tel: (0356) 647283.
A practice area, caddy cars and catering facilities are available (Caddies by arrangement).
Visitors are welcome all week.
Secretary: J.M. Hutchison
Tel: (0356) 647283.
Professional: A.J. Webster
Tel: (0356) 648462.

Elderslie
Renfrewshire

Elderslie Golf Club
63 Main Road, Elderslie.
Tel: Johnstone 22835/23956.
18 holes, length of course 6031 yds.
SSS 69
Charges: £16.10 round, £22 daily.
For advance reservations
Tel: Johnstone 23956.
A practice area and catering facilities are available. Plus P.G.A. professional shop etc.
Secretary: A. Anderson
Tel: Johnstone 23956.

Elgin
Morayshire

Elgin Golf Club
Hardhillock,
Birnie Road,
Elgin IV30 3SX.
Tel: (0343) 542338.
18 holes, length of course 5853m/6401 yds.
SSS 71

Charges: Weekdays: £14 round, £20 daily. Weekends: £20 round, £28 daily.
For advance reservations
Tel: (0343) 542338.
Caddies (by arrangement), caddy cars, and practice area.
Catering facilities are available.
Visitors are welcome.
Secretary: Derek J. Chambers
Tel: (0343) 542338.
Professional: Ian Rodger
Tel: (0343) 542884.

Elie
Fife

Earlsferry Thistle Golf Club
Melon Park.
Tel: Anstruther 310053.
(Further details on application).

The Golf House Club'
Elie, Fife KY9 1AS.
Tel: (0333) 330301.
18 holes, length of course 6241 yds.
SSS 70
Charges: Mon-Fri £22 round, £30 daily. Sat/Sun £33 round, £42 daily.
For advance reservations
Tel: (0333) 330301.
Catering facilities are available.
Visitors are welcome midweek.
Secretary: A. Sneddon
Tel: (0333) 330301.
Professional: Robin Wilson
Tel: (0333) 330955.

Ellon
Aberdeenshire

McDonald Golf Club
Hospital Road, Ellon.
Tel: (0358) 20576.
18 holes.
SSS 69
Charges: Mon-Fri £14, Sat £16, Sun £20.
Catering facilities available on request.
Secretary: Ken Clouston
Tel: (0358) 20576.
Professional: Ronnie Urquhart
Tel: (0358) 22891.

Eyemouth
Berwickshire

Eyemouth Golf Club
(Further details on application).

Falkirk
Stirlingshire

Falkirk Golf Club
Stirling Road,
Camelon, Falkirk.
Tel: (0324) 611061/612219.
18 holes, length of course 6267 yds.
SSS 69
Charges: £10 round, £15 daily.
Advance reservations by arrangement with starter
Tel: (0324) 612219.
A practice area and catering facilities are available.
Visitors are welcome Monday to Friday up to 4.00 pm, (Parties - Mon/Tues/Thurs/Fri/Sun).
Secretary: J. Elliott
Tel: (0324) 34118 (Home).

*Grangemouth Golf Course
Polmont Hill, By Polmont.
Tel: Polmont 711500.
(Further details on application).

Falkland
Fife

Falkland Golf Course
The Myre, Falkland.
Tel: Falkland 57404.
9 holes, length of course 2384m/2608 yds.
SSS 66 (18)
Charges: £7 daily (Mon-Fri), £10 (Sat/Sun).
Visitors are welcome. Parties are welcome by prior arrangement.
Secretary: Mrs. H.H. Horsburgh
Tel: Glenrothes 756075.

Fauldhouse
West Lothian

Greenburn Golf Club
Greenburn, Bridge Street, Fauldhouse.
Tel: (0501) 70292.
(Further details on application).

Fochabers
Morayshire

Garmouth & Kingston Golf Club
Garmouth, Fochabers.
Tel: (0343) 87388.
18 holes, length of course 5656 yds.
SSS 67

Charges: Mon-Fri £10 round, £12 daily. Weekends £14 round, £18 daily. Reduced charges for parties over 12.
For advance reservations
Tel: (0343) 87231.
Catering facilities are available.
Visitors are welcome all week.
Secretary: A. Robertson
Tel: (0343) 87231.

Forfar
Angus

Forfar Golf Club
Cunninghill, Arbroath Road, Forfar DD8 2RL.
Tel: (0307) 462120.
18 holes, length of course 5497m/6108 yds.
SSS 69
Charges: £15 round (Mon-Fri), £20 daily. £25 daily Sat/Sun.
For advance reservations
Tel: (0307) 463773.
A practice area, caddy cars and catering facilities are available.
Visitors are welcome all week.
Managing Secretary: W. Baird
Tel: (0307) 463773.
Professional: Mr. P. McNiven
Tel: (0307) 465683.

Forres
Morayshire

Forres Golf Club
Muiryshade,
Forres IV36 0RD.
Tel: (0309) 672949.
18 holes, length of course 5615m/6141 yds.
SSS 69
Charges: £12 daily, £17 weekends.
For advance reservations
Tel: (0309) 672949.
Caddy cars, practice area and catering facilities are available.
Visitors are welcome all week.
Secretary: D.F. Black
Tel: (0309) 672949.
Professional: Sandy Aird
Tel: (0309) 672250.

Fort Augustus
Inverness-shire

Fort Augustus Golf Club
Markethill, Fort Augustus.
Tel: Fort Augustus 6460.
9 holes (18 tees), length of course 5454 yds.

SSS 68
Charges: £4 daily.
For advance reservations
Tel: Fort Augustus 6460.
Caddy cars available.
Visitors are welcome all week, except Saturday afternoons.
Secretary: I.D. Aitchison
Tel: Fort Augustus 6460.

Fortrose
Ross-shire

Fortrose & Rosemarkie Golf Club
Ness Road East,
Fortrose IV10 8SE.
Tel: Fortrose 20529.
18 holes, length of course 5858 yds.
SSS 69
Charges: £12 per round Mon-Fri; £17 per round Sat/Sun. £17 daily Mon-Fri. £45 5-day ticket.
For advance reservations Tel: Fortrose 20529 (parties only).
A practice area and caddy car available.
Visitors are welcome all week.
Secretary: Margaret Collier - Tel: Fortrose 20529.
Professional: Mr. Graham Philp Tel: Fortrose 20733.

Fort William
Inverness-shire

Fort William Golf Club
North Road, Torlundy,
Fort William.
Tel: (0397) 704464.
18 holes, length of course 6217 yds.
SSS 71
Charges: £8 round, £10 daily.
Bar snacks available.
Visitors are welcome all week.
Secretary: Mr. J. Allan.

Fraserburgh
Aberdeenshire

Fraserburgh Golf Club
Philorth, Fraserburgh.
Tel: (0346) 28287.
18 holes, length of course 6279 yds.
SSS 70
Charges: £11 daily (Mon-Fri), £15 (Sat/Sun), £44 weekly.
A practice area and catering facilities are available.

Secretary: Mr. J. Grant
Tel: (0346) 582978.

Gailes
by Irvine, Ayrshire

Glasgow Golf Club
Gailes, Irvine.
Tel: (0294) 311347.
18 holes, length of course 5937m/6493 yds.
SSS 71
Charges: £25 round, £30 daily (to be reviewed in December). 25% deposit required.
For advance reservations
Tel: 041-942 2011.
A practice area, caddy cars and catering facilities are available.
Caddies available by prior arrangement.
Visitors are welcome Monday to Friday (Prior arrangement for parties of more than 8 players).
Professional: Mr. J. Steven
Tel: 041-942 8507.

Gairloch
Ross-shire

Gairloch Golf Club
Gairloch IV21 2BQ.
Tel: (0445) 2407.
9 holes, length of course (18 holes) 4250 yds.
SSS 63
Charges: £10 daily, £45 weekly. £5 daily for OAP's/juniors.
Caddy cars are available. Club hire.
Visitors are welcome all week.
Secretary: A. Shinkins
Tel: 044 586 346.

Galashiels
Selkirkshire

Galashiels Golf Club
Ladhope Re-creation Ground, Galashiels.
Tel: (0896) 3724.
18 holes, length of course 5185 yds.
SSS 66
Charges: £8 Mon-Fri, £12 Sat & Sun per round. Daily - £12 Mon-Fri, £16 Sat & Sun.
For advance reservations
Tel: (0896) 3724.
A practice area and catering facilities (by arrangement only)

are available.
Visitors are welcome all week (by arrangement).
Secretary: R. Gass
Tel: (0896) 55307.

Torwoodlee Golf Club
Edinburgh Road, Galashiels.
Tel: Galashiels 2260.
9 holes, length of course 5800 yds.
Charges: £12 round, £15 daily.
A practice area, caddy cars and catering facilities are available.
Visitors are welcome all week, except Saturdays to 5.00 pm and Thursdays after 2.00pm.
Secretary: A. Wilson
Tel: (0896) 2260.

Galston
Ayrshire

Loudoun Gowf Club
Galston.
Tel: (0563) 821993.
(Further details on application).

Gatehouse of Fleet
Kirkcudbrightshire

Gatehouse Golf Club
Gatehouse of Fleet.
Tel: Gatehouse 814459.
(Further details on application).

Gifford
East Lothian

Gifford Golf Club
c/o Secretary, Calroust,
Tweeddale Avenue,
Gifford EH41 4QN.
Tel: Gifford 267.
9 and 11 Tees, length of course 6101 yds.
SSS 69
Charges: £10 round/daily (Mon-Sun).
A small practice area is available.
Visitors welcome, except Tuesdays and Wednesdays from 4.00 pm, Saturdays and Sundays from 12 noon. Course closed all day first Sunday each month - April to October.
Secretary: D.A. Fantom
Tel: Gifford 267.

Girvan
Ayrshire

Brunston Castle Golf Club,
Dailly, by Girvan.
Tel: (0465) 81 471.
18 holes, length of course 6792 yds.
SSS 72
Charges: Mon-Fri £20,
Weekends £25 per round. Daily
- £30 Mon-Fri, Weekends £35.
For advance reservations
Tel: (0465) 81 471.
Caddy cars/motor buggies, practice area and catering facilities are available.
Visitors are welcome all week.
Secretary: Ian F. Tennant.
Professional: Douglas Smart
Tel: (0465) 81 471.

Girvan Golf Club
Golf Course Road, Girvan.
Tel: Girvan 4346.
18 holes, length of course 5095 yds.
SSS 65
Charges: £10 round. £18 daily.
Trolleys are available. Catering facilties can be arranged Tel: Girvan 4272.
Visitors are welcome all week.
Secretary: W.B. Tait.

Glasgow

*Alexandra Golf Course
Alexandra Park,
Dennistoun, Glasgow.
Tel: 041-556 3991.
9 holes, length of course 2870 yds.
Charges: Summer - adults £2.05, juveniles 90p, passport to recreation holders 60p. Winter prices: adults - £1.70, juveniles 90p, passport to recreation holders 60p.
For advance reservations
Tel: 041-556 3991.
A practice and catering area are available.
Visitors are welcome all week.
Secretary: R. Watt.

Bishopbriggs Golf Club
Brackenbrae Road,
Bishopbriggs,
Glasgow G64 2DX.
Tel: 041-772 1810.
18 holes, length of course 6041 yds.

SSS 69
Charges: On application.
Catering facilities are available.
Parties are welcome with reservation, Tues & Thurs only (apply to secretary at least one month in advance).
Secretary: John Magin
Tel: 041-772 8938.

Cathcart Castle Golf Club
Mearns Road,
Glasgow G76 7YL.
Tel: 041-638 9449.
18 holes, length of course 5330m/5832 yds.
(Further details on application)

Cawder Golf Club
Cadder Road,
Bishopbriggs.
2 x 18 holes, length of course Cawder 5711m/6244 yds, Keir 5373m/5885 yds.
SSS 71 & 68
Charges: £22 daily.
For advance reservations
Tel: 041-772 5167.
A practice area, caddy cars and catering facilities are available.
Visitors are welcome Monday to Friday.
Secretary: G.T. Stoddart
Tel: 041-772 5167.
Professional: K. Stevely
Tel: 041-772 7102.

Cowglen Golf Club
301 Barrhead Road,
Glasgow G43.
Tel: 041-632 0556.
(Further details on application).

Crow Wood Golf Club
Garnkirk Estate,
Muirhead, Chryston G69 9JF.
Tel: 041-779 2011.
(Further details on application).

*Deaconsbank Golf Course
Rouken Glen Golf Centre,
Stewarton Road,
(Junction A726),
Thornliebank,
Giffnock G46 7UZ.
Tel: 041-638 7044
or 041-620 0826.
18 holes, length of course 4800 yds.
SSS 63 (Par 64).
Charges: Mon-Fri £6, Sat/Sun £7. Day ticket £10 & £12.
Catering facilities are available.
15 bay floodlit driving range,

shop facilities and hiring of clubs, etc.
Visitors are welcome.
Secretary: Christine Cosh.

Glasgow Golf Club
Killermont,
Bearsden, Glasgow.
Tel: 041-942 2011.
18 holes, length of course 5456m/5968 yds.
SSS 69
Charges: On Application.
Visitors by member's introduction on weekdays only.
Professional: Jack Steven
Tel: 041-942 8507.

Haggs Castle Golf Club
70 Dumbreck Road,
Glasgow G41 4SN.
Tel: 041-427 1157.
18 holes, length of course 6464 yds.
SSS 71
Charges: £24 round, £36 daily.
For advance reservations
Tel: 041-427 1157.
A practice area, caddy cars and catering facilities are available.
Visitors must be introduced by a member. Parties only on Wednesdays.
Secretary: Ian Harvey
Tel: 041-427 1157.
Professional: J. McAlister
Tel: 041-427 3355.

Kings Park Golf Course
Carmunnock Road,
Glasgow G44.
9 holes
Charges: Monday to Friday -
Adults: £1.65, Juveniles: £0.85,
Passport to recreation holders:
£0.55. Sat & Sun - Adults:
£1.95, Juveniles: £0.85,
Passport to recreation holders:
£0.55.
(For further information contact the Golf Manager on 041-554 8274.)

*Knightswood Golf Course
Chaplet Avenue,
Glasgow G13.
Tel: 041-959 2131.
9 holes
Charges: Monday to Friday -
Adults: £1.65, Juveniles: £0.85,
Passport to recreation holders:
£0.55. Sat & Sun £1.95 all categories.
(Further details on application).

*Lethamhill Golf Course
Hogganfield Loch,
Cumbernauld Road,
Glasgow G33 1AH.
Tel: 041-770 6220.
18 holes.
Charges: Monday to Friday -
Adults: £3.25, Juveniles: £1.85,
Passport to recreation holders:
£1.15. Sat & Sun £3.80 all categories.
(Further details on application).

*Linn Park Golf Course
Simshill Road,
Glasgow G44 5TA.
Tel: 041-637 5871.
18 holes.
Charges: Monday to Friday -
Adults: £3.25, Juveniles: £1.85,
Passport to recreation holders:
£1.15. Sat & Sun £3.80 all categories.
For advance reservations
Tel: 041-637 5871.

*Littlehill Golf Course
Auchinairn Road,
Glasgow G64 1OT.
Tel: 041-772 1916.
18 holes.
Charges: Monday to Friday -
Adults: £3.25, Juveniles: £1.85,
Passport to recreation holders:
£1.15. Sat & Sun £3.80 all categories.

Mount Ellen Golf Club
Johnstone House,
Johnstone Road, Gartcosh.
Tel: Glenboig 872277.
18 holes, length of course 5525 yds.
SSS 68
Charges: £6 round, £16 daily (package deal). New offer to casual visitor - Mon-Fri, £5.00 per round, £8.00 per day (8.30 am-4.30 pm).
For advance reservations
Tel: Glenboig 872277.
Catering facilities are available.
Visitors are welcome all week.
Secretary: W.J. Dickson.

Pollock Golf Club
90 Barrhead Road,
Glasgow.
Tel: 041-632 4351/1080.
(Further details on application).

*Ruchill Golf Course
Bilsland Drive,
Glasgow G22.
9 holes.
Charges: Monday to Friday -
Adults: £1.65, Juveniles: £0.85,
Passport to recreation holders:
£0.55. Sat & Sun - Adults:
£1.95, Juveniles: £0.85,
Passport to recreation holders:
£0.55.
For further information contact the Golf Manager on 041-554 8274.

The Williamwood Golf Club
Clarkston Road,
Glasgow G44.
Tel: 041-637 1783.
18 holes, length of course 5878 yds.
SSS 68
Charges: on application
Visitors are welcome only when introduced by, and playing with members.
Secretary: R.G. Cuthbert
Tel: 041-226 4311.
Professional: J. Gardner
Tel: 041-637 2715.

Glenluce
Wigtownshire

Wigtownshire County Golf Club
Mains of Park, Glenluce,
Newton Stewart.
Tel: Glenluce 420.
18 holes, length of course 5324m/5823 yds.
SSS 68
Charges: £12 per round, £16 daily (weekdays); £14 per round, £18 daily (Sat/Sun & Bank Hols.).
For advance reservations
Tel: 058 13 420.
Catering facilities are available.
Visitors are welcome all week except Wednesdays after 5.30 pm.
Secretary: R. McKnight
Tel: 058 13 532.

Glenrothes
Fife

Balbirnie Park Golf Club
Balbirnie Park, Markinch,
by Glenrothes, KY7 6DD.
Tel: (0592) 752006.
18 holes, length of course
6210 yds.
SSS 70
Charges: On Application.
For advance reservations
contact: A.D. Gordon, Assistant
Secretary, Tel: (0592) 752006.
Catering facilities by arrange-
ment, contact Club Steward,
Trevor Filshie.
Visitors are welcome all week.
Secretary: A.G. Grant
Tel. (0592) 757114.

Glenrothes Golf Club
Golf Course Road, Glenrothes.
Tel: (0592) 758686.
Length of course
5984m/6444 yds.
SSS 71
Charges: £8 round, £13.50 daily
(weekday), £10 round, £15.50
daily (weekend).
Starter: Tel: (0592) 756941.
For advance reservations Tel:
0592 756941 (Evenings), min.
12 players.
A practice area and catering
facilities are available.
Visitors are welcome all week.
Secretary: Mrs. P.V. Landells
Tel: (0592) 756941.

Glenshee (Spittal o')
Perthshire

Dalmunzie Golf Course
Tel: (0250) 885224.
9 holes, length of course
2036 yds.
SSS 60
Charges: £7.50 daily. Under-
14's half price, under-7's free.
Weekly family ticket £60.
Catering and accommodation
available.

Golspie
Sutherland

Golspie Golf Club
Ferry Road, Golspie.
Tel: (0408) 633266.
18 holes, length of course
5337m/5836 yds.
SSS 68 (Gents)
SSS 71 (Ladies)
Charges: £15 daily, £75 weekly.
Parties must book in advance.
A practice area, caddy cars and
catering facilities are available.
Secretary: Mrs. Marie
MacLeod.

Gourock
Renfrewshire

Gourock Golf Club
Cowal View, Gourock.
Tel: Gourock 31001.
18 holes, length of course
5936m/6492 yds.
SSS 71
Charges: On application.
A practice area and catering
facilities are available.
Visitors are welcome Monday
to Friday.
Secretary: Mr. C.M. Campbell
Tel: Gourock 31001.
Professional: Mr. A. Green
Tel: 36834.

Grantown on Spey
Morayshire

Grantown on Spey Golf Club
The Clubhouse,
Grantown-on-Spey.
Tel: (0479) 2079.
18 holes, length of course
5631 yds.
SSS 67
Charges: £13 per day, £16
weekends, £50 weekly.
For advance reservations
Tel: (0479) 2715/2079.
Caddy cars, practice area and
catering facilities are available.
Visitors are welcome all week.
Secretary: Dennis Elms
Tel: (0479) 2715.

Greenock
Renfrewshire

Greenock Golf Club
Forsyth Street, Greenock
PA16 8RE.
Tel: (0475) 20793.
27 holes, length of course
5888 yds.
SSS 68
Charges: £12 round, £15 daily.
For advance reservations
Tel: (0475) 87236.
A practice area, caddy cars and
catering facilities are available.
Visitors are welcome Tuesday,
Thursday and Sunday.
Secretary: E.J. Black
Tel: (0475) 20793.

Gullane
East Lothian

Gullane No. 1 Golf Course
East Lothian EH31 2BB.
Tel: (0620) 842255.
18 holes, length of course
5913m/6466 yds.
SSS 71
Charges: £35 (Mon-Fri), £45
(Sat/Sun) round, £50 daily
(Mon-Fri). (1993 rates).
For advance reservations
Tel: (0620) 84 2255.
Caddy cars, caddies and
catering facilities are available.
Secretary: A.J.B. Taylor
Tel: (0620) 842255.
Professional: J. Hume
Tel: (0620) 843111.

Gullane No. 2 Golf Course
East Lothian EH31 2BB.
Tel: (0620) 842255.
18 holes, length of course
6244 yds.
SSS 70
Charges: £16 round (Mon-Fri),
£20 (Sat/Sun). £24 daily (Mon-
Fri), £30 (Sat/Sun) (1993 rates).
For advance reservations
Tel: (0620) 842255.
Caddy cars, caddies and
catering facilities are available.
Secretary: A.J.B. Taylor
Tel: (0620) 842255.
Professional: J. Hume
Tel: (0620) 843111.

Gullane No. 3 Golf Course
East Lothian EH31 2BB.
Tel: (0620) 842255.
18 holes, length of course
5166 yds.
SSS 65
Charges: £10 round (Mon-Fri),
£12 (Sat/Sun). £15 daily (Mon-
Fri), £18 (Sat/Sun) (1993 rates).
For advance reservations
Tel: (0620) 842255.
Caddy cars, caddies and
catering facilities are available.
Secretary: A.J.B. Taylor
Tel: (0620) 842255.
Professional: J. Hume
Tel: (0620) 843111.

The Honourable Company of Edinburgh Golfers
Muirfield, Gullane,
East Lothian EH31 2EG.
Tel: (0620) 842123.
18 holes, length of course
6601 yds.
SSS 73
Charges: £48 round, £60 daily
(1993).
For advance reservations
Tel: (0620) 842123.
Caddies, caddy cars, practice
area and catering facilities are
available.
Visitors are welcome, but check
with club. Secretary: Group
Captain J.A. Prideaux
Tel: (0620) 842123.

Haddington
East Lothian

Haddington Golf Club
Amisfield Park, Haddington.
Tel: 062 082 3627/2727.
18 holes, length of course
5764m/6280 yds.
SSS 70
Charges: £9.25 round (Mon-
Fri), £12 (weekends). £12.75
daily (Mon-Fri), £16 (week-
ends).
For advance reservations
Tel: 062 082 2727.
A practice area, caddy cars and
catering facilities are available.
Visitors are welcome all week.
Secretary: A.S.F. Watt
Tel: 062 082 3627.
Professional: J. Sandilands
Tel: 062 082 2727.

Hamilton
Lanarkshire

Hamilton Golf Club
(Further details on application).

*Strathclyde Park Golf Club
Motehill, Hamilton.
Tel: (0698) 266155 (ask for golf
course)
9 holes, length of course
3147 yds.
SSS 70
Charges: £2.25 per round.
For advance reservations: same
day booking only - lines open
8.45am - Tel: (0698) 266155
(ask for golf course).
A practice area and catering
facilities are available.
Visitors are welcome all week.
Secretary: Kevin Will
Tel: (0698) 825363.
Professional: Ken Davidson
Tel: (0698) 283394.

Hawick
Roxburghshire

Minto Golf Club
Denholm, Hawick.
Tel: (0450) 87220.
18 holes, length of course
4992m/5460 yds.
SSS 68
Charges: Weekdays £12 per
round, £18 per day. Weekends
£18 per round, £25 per day.
For advance reservations
Tel: (0450) 87 220.
A practice area, caddy cars and
catering facilities are available.
Visitors are welcome all week.
Secretary: Dr. Ian Todd
Tel: (0450) 72180.

Helensburgh
Dunbartonshire

Helensburgh Golf Club
25 East Abercromby Street,
Helensburgh.
Tel: (0436) 74173.
(Further details on application).

Helmsdale
Sutherland

Helmsdale Golf Club
Golf Road,
Helmsdale KW8 6JA.
Tel: 043 12 240.
9 holes, length of course
3338m/3650 yds (2 x 9 holes).
SSS 62
Charges: £3 round £5 daily, £15

weekly.
For advance reservations
Tel: 043 12 240.
Visitors are welcome all week.
Secretary: Mr. J. Mackay
Tel: 043 12 240.

Hopeman
Morayshire

Hopeman Golf Club
Hopeman, Elgin,
Morayshire.
Tel: (0343) 830578.
18 holes, length of course
5003m/5474 yds.
SSS 67
Charges: Daily (Mon-Fri), £10,
after 3pm £7. (Sat-Sun), £15,
after 3pm £10. 5-day ticket
(Mon-Fri) £30, 7-day consecu-
tive ticket £40.
For advance reservations
Tel: (0343) 830578.
A small practice area and
catering facilities are available.
Visitors are welcome all week.
Secretary: W.H. Dunbar
Tel: (0343) 830687.

Huntly
Aberdeenshire

Huntly Golf Club
Cooper Park, Huntly.
Tel: (0466) 792643.
18 holes, length of course
5399 yds.
SSS 66.
Charges: £10 (weekdays) £15
(weekends) daily.
Catering facilities are available.
Secretary: G. Alexander.

Innellan
Argyll

Innellan Golf Club
Innellan.
Tel: Innellan 242.
9 holes, length of course 18
holes 4246m/4642 yds.
Charges: £4 (Mon-Sat), £5 Sun
per round. £4 (Mon-Sat), £5 Sun
daily. Weekly £12.
Catering facilities are available.
Visitors are welcome all week,
except Mon, Tues and Wed
from 5 pm.
Secretary: Jeff Arden
Tel: Dunoon 3546.

Innerleithen
Peeblesshire

Innerleithen Golf Club
Leithen Water.
9 holes, length of course
5984 yds.
SSS 68
Charges: £8 daily Mon-Fri, £10
daily weekends.
Secretary: S.C. Wyse
Tel: Innerleithen 830071.

Insch
Aberdeenshire

Insch Golf Club
Golf Terrace,
Insch, Aberdeenshire.
Tel: (0464) 20363.
9 holes, length of course: men's
5,632 yds. Ladies 4,972 yds.
SSS 67 men's
SSS 69 Ladies
Charges: Mon-Fri £7 per round/
daily. £9 Sat & Sun per round/
daily.
For advance reservations Tel:
(0464) 20291.
Caddies, caddy cars and
catering facilities are available.
Visitors are welcome Mon, Tues
& Wed; Tee reserved from 4pm.
Secretary: James G. McCombie
Tel: (0464) 20291.

Inverallochy
Aberdeenshire

Inverallochy Golf Course
24 Shore Street, Cairnbulg.
Tel: Inverallochy 2324.
18 holes, length of course
5137 yds. Par 64.
(Further details on application).

Invergordon
Ross-shire

Invergordon Golf Club
(Further details on application).

Inverness
Inverness-shire

Inverness Golf Club
Culcabock Road,
Inverness IV2 3XQ.
Tel: (0463) 239882.
18 holes, length of course
5694m/6226 yds.
SSS 70

Charges: £15 round, £20 day
ticket (weekdays). £18 round,
£22 day ticket (Sat/Sun &
public holidays). £60 weekly
ticket.
For advance reservations
Tel: (0463) 239882 or 231989.
A practice area, caddy cars,
caddies and catering facilities
are available.
Visitors are welcome all week
(restrictions on Saturdays).
Secretary: J. McGill.
Professional: A.P. Thomson
Tel: (0463) 231989.

Torvean Golf Club
Glenurquhart Road,
Inverness.
Tel: (0463) 225651.
18 holes, length of course
5784 yds.
SSS 69
Charges: £8.20 (weekdays),
£9.50 (weekends) per round.
£10.90 (weekdays), £12.30
(weekends) daily.
For advance reservations
Tel: (0463) 711434.
A practice area is available.
Visitors are welcome all week -
but booking is advisable.
Secretary: Mrs. K.M. Gray
Tel: (0463) 225651.

Inverurie
Aberdeenshire

Inverurie Golf Club
Davah Wood,
Blackhall Road, Inverurie.
Tel: Inverurie 20207/24080.
18 holes, length of course
5096 yds.
SSS 66
Charges: £10 daily (Mon-Fri),
£15 (Sat/Sun).
A practice area (for members
only), caddy cars and catering
facilities are available.
Administrator: Mrs. A. Gerrard
Tel: Inverurie 24080.

Irvine
Ayrshire

The Irvine Golf Club
Bogside, Irvine.
Tel: (0294) 75979.
18 holes, length of course
5858m/6408 yds.
SSS 71
Charges: £23 round, £28 daily.

For advance reservations
Tel: (0294) 75979.
A practice area, caddy cars and
catering facilities are available
(Caddies by arrangement).
Visitors are welcome by
arrangement.
Secretary: Mr. Andrew Morton
Tel: (0294) 75979.
Professional: Mr. Keith Erskine
Tel: Irvine 75626.

*Ravenspark Golf Course
Kidsneuk.
Tel: Irvine 79550.
(Further details on application).

Jedburgh
Roxburghshire

Jedburgh Golf Club
Dunion Road, Jedburgh.
Tel: (0835) 63587.
9 holes, length of course
2746m/5492 yds.
SSS 67
Charges: £10 daily.
For advance reservations
Tel: (0835) 63587 (evenings).
Catering facilities are available.
Visitors are welcome all week.
Secretary: R. Strachan.

Johnstone
Renfrewshire

Cochrane Castle Golf Club
Craigston, Johnstone PA5 0HF.
Tel: (0505) 20146.
18 holes, length of course
6226 yds.
SSS 70
Charges: £15 (round), £20
(daily).
Advance reservations by letter
only.
Caddy cars, a practice area and
catering facilities are available.
Visitors are welcome Monday
to Friday.
Secretary: J.C. Cowan
Tel: (0505) 20146.
Professional:
Stuart H. Campbell
Tel: (0505) 28465.

Keith
Banffshire

Keith Golf Course
Fife Park.
Tel: Keith 2469.
(Further details on application).

Kelso
Roxburghshire

Kelso Golf Club
Racecourse Road, Kelso.
Tel: (0573) 23009.
(Further details on application).

Kemnay
Aberdeenshire

Kemnay Golf Club
Monymusk Road, Kemnay.
Tel: (0467) 42225.
9 holes.
SSS 67
Charges: £8 daily, £10
weekends.
For advance reservations
Tel: (0467) 42225.
Limited Catering available from
the bar.
Visitors are welcome Sundays,
depending on starting times.
Secretary: Mr. D.W. Imrie
Tel: (0467) 43047.

Kenmore
Perthshire

Kenmore Golf Course,
Mains of Taymouth, Kenmore.
Tel: (0887) 830226.
9 holes, length of course
2751m/3026 yds.
18 holes, length of course
5502m/6052 yds.
SSS 69
Charges: £10 adults, £7 juniors
round. £15 adults, £11 juniors
daily. £40 adults, £30 juniors
weekly.
For advance reservations
Tel: (0887) 830226.
Practice area, caddy cars and
catering facilities are available.
Visitors are welcome all week.
Secretary: Robin Menzies
Tel: (0887) 830226.

**Taymouth Castle Golf
Course**
Kenmore, Tayside PH15 2NT.
Tel: (0887) 830228.
18 holes, length of course
6066 yds.
Mens Medal Tees SSS 69
Yellow Tees SSS 67
Ladies SSS 72
Charges: Weekday £14,
weekend & Bank Hols. £18
(round). Weekdays £22 (daily).
For advance reservations - Mike

Mulcahey Tel: (0887) 830228.
Caddy cars, a practice area and
catering facilities are available.
Visitors are welcome all week
with reservations.
Professional: Alex Marshall
Tel: (0887) 820910.

Kilbirnie
Ayrshire

Kilbirnie Place Golf Club
Largs Road, Kilbirnie.
Tel: Kilbirnie 683398.
18 holes, length of course
5500 yds.
SSS 67
Charges: £10 weekday, £17.50
Sunday (round). £15 weekday
(daily).
Catering facilities are available.
Visitors are welcome, except
Saturdays.
Secretary: J.C. Walker
Tel Kilbirnie 683283.

Killin
Perthshire

Killin Golf Club
Killin Golf Course
Killin.
Tel: (0567) 820312.
9 holes, length of course
2410 yds.
SSS 65
Charges: Round £9, £12 daily.
Caddy cars and catering
facilities are available.
Visitors are welcome all week.
Secretary: Mr. A. Chisholm
Tel: 08383 235.

Kilmacolm
Renfrewshire

Kilmacolm Golf Club
Porterfield Road,
Kilmacolm.
Tel: Kilmacolm 2139.
18 holes, length of course
5890 yds.
SSS 68
Charges: £15 per round, £20
daily.
Caddy cars, a practice area and
catering facilities are available.
Visitors are welcome on
weekdays.
Professional: D. Stewart
Tel: 2695.

Kilmarnock
Ayrshire

*Caprington Golf Club
Ayr Road, Kilmarnock.
Tel: Kilmarnock 21915.
(Further details on application).

Kilspindie
East Lothian

Kilspindie Golf Club
Aberlady,
East Lothian EH32 0QD.
Tel: Aberlady 216 or 358.
18 holes, length of course
4957m/5410 yds.
SSS 66
Charges: £16 round (Mon-Fri),
£20 (Sat/Sun), £20 daily (Mon-
Fri), £26 (Sat/Sun).
A practice area, caddy cars and
catering facilities are available.
Visitors are welcome Monday
to Friday.
Secretary: H.F. Brown
Tel: Aberlady 358.

Kilsyth
Stirlingshire

Kilsyth Lennox Golf Club
Tak-Ma-Doon Road,
Kilsyth, G65 0HX.
Tel: Kilsyth 822190.
9 holes, length of course
5934 yds.
SSS 69
Charges: £6 round, £10 daily.
Catering facilities are available.
Visitors are welcome all week
with reservation.
Secretary: A.G. Stevenson

Kincardine on Forth
Fife

Tulliallan Golf Club
Alloa Road,
Kincardine-on-Forth.
Tel: Kincardine-on-Forth
30396.
18 holes, length of course
5459m/5965 yds.
SSS 69
Charges: £14 round (Mon·Fri),
£16 (Sat/Sun), £18.50 daily
(Mon·Fri), £23 (Sat/Sun).
For advance reservations
Tel: (0259) 30798.
Caddy cars and catering
facilities are available.
Visitors are welcome by prior
arrangement.

Secretary: J.S. McDowall
Tel: (0324) 485420.
Professional: Steve Kelly
Tel: (0259) 730798.

Kingarth
Isle of Bute

Bute Golf Club
Kingarth.
9 holes, length of course
2284m/2497 yds.
SSS 64
Charges: Adults £5 daily, £15
weekly. Juniors (under-17 yrs)
£1 daily, £5 pa + £5 joining fee.
Secretary: J. Burnside.

Kinghorn
Fife

***Kinghorn Municipal Golf
Club**
c/o Kirkcaldy District Council,
Leisure & Direct Services
Division,
Kinghorn.
Tel: (0592) 645000.
18 holes, length of course
4544m/4969 yds.
SSS 67
(Par 65)
Charges: £7.60 round (Mon-
Fri), £10 (Sat/Sun) (1992).
Catering facilites through
Clubmistress
Tel: Kinghorn 890345.
Secretary: J.P. Robertson
Tel: (0592) 203397.

Kingussie
Inverness-shire

Kingussie Golf Club
Gynack Road, Kingussie.
Tel: Clubhouse - Kingussie
661374
Sec. Office - Kingussie 661600.
18 holes, length of course
5079m/5555 yds.
SSS 67
Charges: Weekdays £10.50
round, £13.50 daily; Sat/Sun
£12.50 round, £16.50 daily. £47
weekly (1993).
For advance reservations
Tel: Kingussie 661600/661374.
Caddy cars and catering
facilities are available.
Visitors are welcome all week.
Secretary: N.D. MacWilliam
Tel: Kingussie 661600.

Kinnesswood
Kinross-shire

Bishopshire Golf Course
(Further details on application).

Kinross
Kinross-shire

Green Hotel Golf Courses
Green Hotel.
Tel: (0577) 63467.
Red Course - 18 holes, length of
course 5719m/6257 yds.
SSS 73
Blue Course - 18 holes, length
of course 5905m/6456 yds.
SSS 74
Charges (both courses): £14
round Mon-Fri, £20 Sat/Sun.
£20 daily Mon-Fri, £30 Sat/Sun
(1993).
For advance reservation
Tel: Green Hotel.
Caddy cars and catering
facilities are available.
Secretary: M. Smith.

Kintore
Aberdeenshire

Kintore Golf Club
Balbithan Road, Kintore.
Tel: (0467) 32631.
18 holes, length of course
5974 yds.
SSS 69
Charges: £8 daily, £12
weekends. £6 after 6pm all
week.
For advance reservations
Tel: (0467) 32631.
Visitors are welcome all week
except between 4pm-7pm Mon,
Wed and Fri.
Secretary: J.D. Black
Tel: (0467) 32214.

Kirkcaldy
Fife

***Dunnikier Park Golf
Course**
Dunnikier Way, Kirkcaldy, Fife.
Tel: Kirkcaldy 261599.
18 holes, length of course
6036m/6601 yds.
SSS 72
Charges: £7.60 round, £13 daily
(Mon-Fri); £10 round, £15 daily
(Sat/Sun).
A practice area, caddy cars and
catering facilities are available.
Secretary: Mr. R.A. Waddell.

Kirkcaldy Golf Club
Balwearie Road,
Kirkcaldy, Fife.
Tel: Kirkcaldy 260370.
18 holes, length of course
6004 yds.
SSS 70
Charges: £12 round (weekdays),
£15 (weekends), £18 daily
(weekdays), £21 daily
(weekends).
For advance reservations Tel:
Kirkcaldy 205240/203258.
A practice area, caddy cars and
catering facilities are available.
Visitors are welcome all week,
except Tuesdays and Saturdays.
Secretary: J.I. Brodley - Tel:
Kirkcaldy 205240/263316
(home).
Professional: Mr. Paul Hodgson
Tel: Kirkcaldy 203258.

Kirkcudbright
Kirkcudbrightshire

Kirkcudbright Golf Club
Stirling Crescent,
Kirkcudbright DG6 4EZ.
Tel: (0557) 30314.
18 holes, length of course
5121m/5598 yds.
SSS 67
Charges: £15 round, £20 daily,
£50 weekly.
For advance reservations
Tel: (0557) 30314.
Visitors are welcome all week.
Secretary: J.H. Sommerville
Tel: (0557) 30314.

Kirkintilloch
Dunbartonshire

Hayston Golf Club
Campsie Road,
Kirkintilloch G66 1RN.
Tel: 041-776 1244.
18 holes, length of course
5808m/6042 yds.
SSS 69
Charges: £15 round, £25 daily.
For advance reservations Tel:
041-775 0882.
A practice area, caddy cars and
catering facilities are available.
Secretary: J.V. Carmichael
Tel: 041-775 0723
Professional: Mr. S. Barnett
Tel: 041-775 0882.

Kirkintilloch Golf Club
Todhill, Campsie Road.
Tel: 041-776 1256.
(Further details on application).

Kirkwall
Orkney

Orkney Golf Club
Grainbank.
Tel: (0856) 872487.
18 holes, length of course
5406 yds.
SSS 68
Charges: £10 daily, £35 weekly,
£50 fortnightly.
A practice area is available.
Visitors are welcome all week.
Secretary: L.F. Howard
Tel: (0856) 874165.

Kirriemuir
Angus

Kirriemuir Golf Club
Northmuir, Kirriemuir.
Tel: (0575) 72144.
18 holes, length of course
5553 yds.
SSS 66
Charges: £13 round, £18 daily,
£65 weekly (1993).
Practice area, caddy cars and
catering facilities are available.
Visitors are welcome weekdays.
Professional: Mr. A. Caira
Tel: (0575) 73317.
Fax: (0575) 74608.

Ladybank
Fife

Ladybank Golf Club
Annsmuir, Ladybank, Fife.
Tel: (0337) 30814/30725.
18 holes, length of course
6641 yds.
SSS 72
Charges: Nov/April - £14 per
round, £20 daily. May & Oct. -
£17 per round, £24 daily. June/
Sept. - £23 per round, £31 daily.
Weekly £90.
For advance reservations
Tel: (0337) 30814.
Caddy cars, a practice area and
catering facilities are available.
Visitors are welcome all week,
except Saturdays.
Secretary: A.M. Dick
Tel: (0337) 30814.
Professional: M. Gray
Tel: (0337) 30725.

Lamlash
By Brodick, Isle of Arran

Lamlash Golf Club
Tel: Clubhouse (0770) 600 296.
Starter (0770) 600 196.
18 holes, length of course
4611 yds.
SSS 63
Charges: £9 daily Mon-Fri, £11
Sat/Sun. Weekly £55; Fort-
nightly £80 (1993).
Secretary: J. Henderson
Tel: Lamlash 272.

Lanark
Lanarkshire

Lanark Golf Club
The Moor,
Whitelees Road, Lanark.
Tel: Lanark 3219.
18 hole and 9 hole, length of
course 6423 yds.
SSS 71 (18 hole)
Charges: £18 round, £28 daily.
For advance reservations
Tel: Lanark 662349.
A practice area, caddy cars and
catering facilities are available
(Caddies if requested).
Visitors are welcome Monday
to Thursday.
Secretary: G.H. Cuthill
Tel: Lanark 663219.
Professional: R. Wallace
Tel: Lanark 661456.

Langbank
Renfrewshire

The Gleddoch Club
Langbank,
Renfrewshire PA14 6YE.
Tel: (0475) 54 304.
18 holes, length of course
6332 yds.
SSS 71
Charges: £25 for visitors (day
ticket)
For advance reservations
Tel: (0475) 54304.
Trolleys, practice area, hire or
clubs and catering facilities are
available.
Visitors are welcome all week.
Secretary: Tel: (0475) 54 304.
Professional:
Tel: (0475) 54 704.

Langholm
Dumfriesshire

Langholm Golf Course
Whitaside, Langholm,
Dumfriesshire.
9 holes, length of course
5744 yds.
SSS 68
Charges: £8 round/daily, £30
weekly.
Practice area is available.
Visitors are welcome all week.
Secretary: C.A. Edgar
Tel: (03873) 80878.

Larbert
Stirlingshire

Falkirk Tryst Golf Club
86 Burnhead Road,
Stenhousemuir,
Larbert FK5 4BD.
Tel: (0324) 562415.
18 holes, length of course
5533m/6083 yds
SSS 69
Charges: £11 round, £16 daily.
For advance reservations
Tel: (0324) 562054.
Caddy cars, practice area and
catering facilities are available.
No unintroduced visitors on
Saturdays/Sundays.
Secretary: R.D. Wallace
Tel: (0324) 562415/562054.
Professional: Steven Dunsmore
Tel: (0324) 562091.

Glenbervie Golf Club
Stirling Road,
Larbert FK1 4SJ.
Tel: Larbert 562605.
18 holes, length of course
6469 yds.
SSS 71
Charges: £20 round, £30 daily.
For advanced reservations
Tel: Larbert 562605 (visiting
parties).
A practice area, caddy cars and
catering facilities are available.
Visitors are welcome Monday
to Friday.
Secretary: Mrs. M. Purves
Tel: Larbert 562605.
Professional: Mr. J. Chillas
Tel: Larbert 562725.

Largs
Ayrshire

Largs Golf Club
Irvine Road,
Largs KA30 8EV.
Tel: (0475) 673594.
18 holes, length of course
6220 yds.
SSS 70
Charges: £18 round, £24 daily.
For advance reservations
Tel: (0475) 686192.
A practice area, caddy cars and
catering facilities are available.
Visitors are welcome all week.
Parties - Tues & Thur.
Secretary: F. Gilmour
Tel: (0475) 672497.
Professional: R. Collinson
Tel: (0475) 686192.

Larkhall
Lanarkshire

*Larkhall Golf Course
(Further details on application).

Lauder
Berwickshire

*Lauder Golf Club
Lauder.
Tel: (0578) 722526.
9 holes, length of course
6002 yds.
SSS 70
Charges: £6 weekdays, £7
weekends.
Practice area is available.
Visitors are welcome all week
(some restrictions before noon
on Sundays and 5pm Wednes-
days).
Secretary: David Dickson
Tel: (0578) 722526.

Lennoxtown
Stirlingshire

Campsie Golf Course
Crow Road.
Tel: Lennoxtown 310244.
(Further details on application).

Lenzie
Lanarkshire

Lenzie Golf Club
19 Crosshill Road.
Tel: 041-776 1535.
(Further details on application).

Lerwick
Shetland

The Shetland Golf Club
Dale Golf Course
P.O. Box 18.
Tel: Gott 369.
18 holes, length of course
5279m/5776 yds.
SSS 70
Charges: £8 daily.
Visitors are welcome.
Secretary: D.C. Gray.

Leslie
Fife

Leslie Golf Club
Balsillie Laws,
Leslie, Glenrothes.
9 holes, length of course
4516m/4940 yds.
SSS 64
Charges: £5 day ticket. £8
Sat./Sun.
Bar facilities from 7.30 pm
11.00 pm.
Visitors are welcome all week.
Secretary: M.G. Burns ·
Tel: (0592) 741449.

Lesmahagow
Lanarkshire

*Hollandbush Golf Club
Acretophead, Lesmahagow.
Tel: Lesmahagow 893484.
(Further details on application).

Leuchars
Fife

St. Michael's Golf Club
Tel: (0334) 839365.
9 holes, length of course
(yellow tees) 5158 yds.
SSS 68, (Par 70).
Charges: £12 day ticket,
under-16's £6.
For Society reservations Tel:
(0334) 55328 (after 6pm).
Caddy cars, bar and catering
facilities are available.
Visitors are welcome all week
but not before 1 pm on Sundays.
Hon. Secretary: Maj. (Retd)
L.M. McIntosh
Tel: (0334) 55328 (Home).

Leven
Fife

Leven Links Golf Course
The Promenade,
Leven KY8 4HS.
Tel: (0333) 428859.
18 holes, length of course
5800m/6400 yds.
SSS 71
Charges: On Application.
For advance reservations
Tel: (0333) 428859.
Catering facilities are available.
Visitors are welcome Sunday to
Friday.
Secretary: B. Jackson, Esq
Tel: (0333) 428859.

Leven Thistle Golf Club
Balfour Street, Leven.
Tel: Leven 26397.
18 holes, length of course
5800m/6434 yds.
SSS 71
Charges: £13 round, £18 daily.
For advance reservations Tel:
Mr. B. Jackson · Leven 428859.
A practice area, caddy cars and
catering facilities are available.
Visitors are welcome Monday
to Friday (Small Parties -
weekend).
Secretary: J. Scott
Tel: Leven 26397.

*Scoonie Golf Club
North Links,
Leven KY8 4SP.
Tel: (0333) 27057.
18 holes, length of course
4967m.
SSS 66
Charges: £8 round, £13.50 daily
weekdays; £10 round, £15.50
daily weekends. Reduction for
OAPs.
Caddy cars and full catering
facilities are available.
Visitors are welcome, except
Thursdays & Saturdays.
Secretary: Mr. Stefan
Kuczerepa - Tel: (0333)
351426.

Linlithgow
West Lothian

Linlithgow Golf Club
Braehead, Linlithgow.
Tel: (0506) 842585.
18 holes, length of course
5239m/5729 yds.
SSS 68

Charges: £10 round, £15 daily (Mon-Fri). £15 round, £20 daily (Sun).
For advance reservations Tel: (0506) 842585.
A practice area, caddy cars and catering facilities are available.
Visitors are welcome all week except Wednesdays and Saturdays.
Secretary: Mrs. A. Bird - Tel: (0506) 842585.
Professional: Mr. T.B. Thomson - Tel: (0506) 844356.

Lochcarron
Ross-shire

Lochcarron Golf Club
Lochcarron, Wester Ross.
Tel: (05202) 257.
9 holes, length of course 1733 yds.
SSS 60
Charges: £5 (round), £8 (daily), £18 (weekly).
Visitors are welcome all week.
Secretary: G. Weighill - Tel: (05202) 257.

Lochgelly
Fife

Lochgelly Golf Course
Lochgelly Golf Club
Cartmore Road Lochgelly.
Tel: Lochgelly 780174.
(Further details on application).

Lochgilphead
Argyllshire

Lochgilphead Golf Club
Blarbuie Road, Lochgilphead.
Tel: (0546) 602340.
9 holes, length of course 4484 yds.
Visitors welcome.
(Further details on application).

Lochmaben
Dumfriesshire

Lochmaben Golf Club
Back Road, Lochmaben,
Lockerbie DG11 1NT.
Tel: (0387) 810552.
9 holes, length of course 4616m/5304 yds.
SSS 66
Charges: £8 round/daily (weekdays), £10 round/daily

(weekends).
A practice area is available.
Catering facilities by special arrangement for visiting parties.
Visitors are welcome weekdays before 5 pm and weekends, except when competitions are in progress.
Secretary: K. Purves
Tel: Annan 3379.

Lochranza
Isle of Arran

Lochranza Golf Course
Isle of Arran KA27 8HL.
Tel/Fax: (0770) 830273.
9 holes, length of course 5500 yds. Par 70
(Further details on application).

Lockerbie
Dumfriesshire

Lockerbie Golf Club
Corrie Road, Lockerbie.
Tel: Lockerbie 203363.
18 holes, length of course 5418 yds.
SSS 66
Charges: £16 Mon-Fri; £20 Sat/Sun daily. £16 per round Sun.
For advance reservations Tel: (0576) 202462.
A practice area and catering facilities are available.
Visitors are welcome all week.
Secretary: J. Thomson
Tel: (0576) 202462.

Lochwinnoch
Renfrewshire

Lochwinnoch Golf Club
Burnfoot Road, Lochwinnoch.
Tel: Lochwinnoch 842153.
Length of course 6243 yds.
SSS 70
Charges: £20 round/daily
For advance reservations write to secretary.
A practice area, caddy cars and catering facilities are available.
Visitors are welcome mid week.
Secretary: Mrs. E. McBride
Tel: 842153.
Prrofessional: Gerry Reilly
Tel: 843029.

Longniddry
East Lothian

Longniddry Golf Club
Links Road,
Longniddry EH32 ONL.
Tel: (0875) 52141.
18 holes, length of course 6219 yds.
SSS 70
Charges: £22 round (Mon-Fri), £32 daily (Mon-Fri).
For advance reservations
Tel: (0875) 52141.
A practice area, caddy cars and catering facilities are available.
Visitors are welcome Mon to Fri.
Secretary: G.C. Dempster
Tel: (0875) 52141.
Professional: W.J. Gray
Tel: (0875) 52228.

Lossiemouth
Morayshire

Moray Golf Club
Stotfield, Lossiemouth.
Tel: (0343) 812018.
18 holes both courses.
Charges: On request.
Caddy cars, practice area and catering facilities are available.
visitors are welcome without reservation.
Secretary: J. Hamilton
Tel: (0343) 812018
Professional: A. Thomson
Tel: (0343) 813330.

Lundin Links
Fife

Lundin Golf Club
Golf Road,
Lundin Links, Leven.
Tel: (0333) 320202.
18 holes, length of course 6377 yds.
SSS 71
Charges: £18 per round (Mon-Fri). £25 (Sats). £27 daily. £80 weekly ticket.
For advance reservations
Tel. (0333) 320202.
Caddy cars, practice area and catering facilities are available.
Visitors are welcome all week, except on Saturdays they cannot play before 2.30pm.

Secretary: A.C. McBride
Tel: (0333) 320202.
Professional: D.K. Webster
Tel: (0333) 320051.

Lundin Ladies Golf Club
Woodlielea Road,
Lindin Links,
Leven KY8 6AR.
9 holes, length of course
2365 yds.
SSS 67
Charges: £6 weekdays (18
holes), £7.50 weekends (18
holes).
For advance reservations
Tel: (0333) 320832 (Clubhouse)
or write to secretary.
A few caddy cars are available.
Visitors are welcome all week.
Secretary: Mrs. Elizabeth
Davidson.

Lybster
Caithness

Lybster Golf Club
Main Street,
Lybster, Caithness.
9 holes, length of course
1807 yds.
SSS 62
Charges: Daily, £4; juniors £2.
Weekly £10.
Advance reservations are not
necessary.
Visitors are welcome all week.
Secretary: Norman S. Fraser.

Macduff
Banffshire

Royal Tarlair Golf Club
Buchan Street, Macduff.
Tel: (0261) 32897.
18 holes, length of course
5866 yds.
SSS 68
Charges: £8 per round
weekdays, £10 per round Sat/
Sun. £12 per day weekdays, £15
per day Sat/Sun. Juniors £5 per
day. Adult weekly ticket £40,
Junior weekly ticket £15.
For advance reservations
Tel: (0261) 32897.
Caddies, caddy cars and
catering facilities are available.
Visitors are welcome all week.
Secretary: Mrs. T. Watt
Tel: (0261) 32897.

Machrie
Isle of Islay

The Machrie Golf Club
The Machrie Hotel & Golf
Club,
Port Ellen, Islay PA42 7AN.
Tel: (0496) 2310.
(Further details on application)

Maddiston
By Falkirk, Stirlingshire

Polmont Golf Club Ltd
Manuel Rigg, Maddiston,
Falkirk FK2 0LS.
Tel: Polmont 711277.
9 holes, length of course
6603 yds.
SSS 70
Charges: Daily - £5 (Mon-Fri),
£10 Sunday.
Catering facilities are available.
Visitors are welcome all week,
except after 5pm and Saturdays.
Secretary: P. Lees
Tel: (0324) 713811.

Mallaig
Inverness-shire

Traigh Golf Club
(Further details on application).

Mauchline
Ayrshire

Ballochmyle Golf Club
Mauchline KA5 6LE.
Tel: (0290) 50469.
18 holes, length of course
5847 yds.
SSS 69
Charges: On application.
Catering facilities are available.
Visitors are welcome with
reservation.
Secretary: D.G. Munro
Tel: (0290) 50469.

Maybole
Ayrshire

*Maybole Golf Course
(Further details on application).

Melrose
Roxburghshire

Melrose Golf Club
The Clubhouse,
Dingleton Road, Melrose.
Tel: Melrose 2855.
(Further details on application).

Millport
Isle of Cumbrae

Millport Golf Club
Golf Road, Millport, Isle of
Cumbrae KA28.
Tel: (0475) 530311.
Length of course 5831 yds.
SSS 68
Charges: On application.
Full catering facilities are
available.
Visitors are welcome all week
without introduction.
Secretary: W.D. Patrick
Tel: (0475) 530-308.
Starter: Tel: (0475) 530305.

Milnathort
Kinross-shire

Milnathort Golf Club Ltd
South Street, Milnathort.
Tel: (0577) 864069.
9 holes, length of course
5669 yds.
SSS 69
Charges: £10 daily (weekdays),
£15 daily (weekends).
For advance reservations
Tel: (0577) 64069.
A practice area is available.
Catering facilities are only
available with prior booking.
Visitors are welcome all week.
Captain: R. Wallace
Tel: (0577) 863855.

Milngavie
Dunbartonshire

Clober Golf Club
Craigton Road,
Milngavie.
Tel: 041-956 6963.
18 holes, length of course
5068 yds.
SSS 65
Charges: £9 per round.
Caddy cars and catering
facilities are available.
Visitors welcome until 4.30pm
Mon to Thurs, 4pm on Fri (last

Tues monthly 4pm).
Secretary: J. Anderson
Tel: 041-956 2499.

Dougalston Golf Course
Strathblane Road,
Milngavie, Glasgow.
Tel: 041·956 5750.
(Further details on application).
Golf Manager: W. McInnes
Tel: 041-956 5750.

Hilton Park Golf Club
Stockmuir Road,
Milngavie, G62 7HB.
Tel: 041-956 4657.
2 x 18 hole courses, length of
courses 6007 and 5374 yds.
SSS 70 and 67
Charges: On application.
Caddy cars, practice area and
catering facilities are available.
Visitors are welcome by prior
arrangement Monday-Thursday,
except 2nd and 4th Tuesdays of
each month.
Secretary: Mrs. J.A. Warnock
Tel: 041·956 4657.
Professional: Mr. Wm.
McCondichie
Tel: 041-956 5125.

Milngavie Golf Club
Laighpark, Milngavie,
Glasgow G62.
Tel: 041·956 1619.
18 holes, length of course
5818 yds.
SSS 68
A practice area and catering
facilities are available.
Visitors are welcome if
introduced by a member.
Secretary: Mrs. A.J.W. Ness
Tel: 041·956 1619.

Moffat
Dumfrieshire

The Moffat Golf Club
Coatshill, Moffat DG10 9SB.
Tel: (0683) 20020.
18 holes, length of course
5218 yds.
SSS 66
Charges: Day tickets -
weekdays £16, weekends £24
(1993).
For advance reservations
Tel: (0683) 20020.
Caddy cars and catering
facilities are available.
Visitors are welcome, except

Wednesday after 12 noon.
Secretary: T.A. Rankin
Tel: (0683) 20020.

Monifieth
Angus

Ashludie Golf Course
The Links, Monifieth.
Tel: (0382) 532767.
18 holes, length of course
5123 yds.
SSS 66
Charges: Weekdays - £14
round, £20 daily; junior £3.50.
Sat/Sun £15 round, £22 daily;
junior £4.50. Weekly £41.
Composite ticket: Mon-Fri £24,
Sat/Sun £28.
For party reservations
Tel: (0382) 535553.
Caddy cars and catering
facilities are available.
Visitors are welcome Monday
to Friday after 9.30am. Saturday
after 2 pm and Sundays after 10
am.
Secretary: H.R. Nicoll
Tel: (0382) 535553.
Professional: Ian McLeod
Tel: (0382) 532945.

Broughty Golf Club
6 Princes Street,
Monifieth, Dundee.
Tel: Monifieth 532147.
For advance reservations
Tel: 0382 532767.
A practice area, caddy cars and
catering facilities are available.
Visitors are welcome all week
and after 2 pm on Saturdays.
Secretary: Samuel J. Gailey ·
Tel: (0382) 730014.
Professional: Ian McLeod
Tel: (0382) 532945.

Medal Course
The Links, Monifieth.
Tel: (0382) 532767.
18 holes, length of course
6657 yds.
SSS 72
Charges: Weekdays: £22 round,
£32 daily; juniors £11. Sat/Sun
£24 round, £36 daily. Weekly
£66.
For party reservations
Tel: (0382) 535553.
Caddy cars and catering
facilities are available.
Visitors are welcome Monday
to Friday after 9.30am, Saturday
after 2pm and Sunday after

10am.
Secretary: H.R. Nicoll
Tel: (0382) 535553.
Professional: Ian McLeod
Tel: (0382) 532945.

Montrose
Angus

Mercantile Golf Club
East Links, Montrose.
Tel: Montrose 72408.
(Further details on application).

Montrose Links Trust
Traill Drive,
Montrose DD10 8SW.
Tel: (0674) 72932.
Medal - 18 holes, length of
course 6443 yds.
Broomfield - 18 holes, length of
course 4765 yds.
SSS 71
SSS 63
Charges: Medal - Mon-Fri £22
daily, £30 Sat & Sun. £13 per
round, £19 Sat & Sun. Weekly
£70.
Broomfield - Mon-Fri £12 daily,
£18 Sat & Sun. £8 per round,
£12 Sat & Sun. Weekly £46.
Reductions for juniors,
members' guests and unem-
ployed.
For advance reservations
Tel: (0674) 72932.
Caddy cars, practice area and
catering facilities are available.
Visitors are welcome all week
on Broomfield Course. No
Saturdays or Sundays before
10am on Medal Course.
Secretary:
Mrs. Margaret Stewart
Tel: (0674) 72932.
Professional: Kevin Stables
Tel: (0674) 72634.

Motherwell
Lanarkshire

Colville Park Golf Club
Jerviston Estate,
Merry Street, Motherwell.
Tel: Motherwell 263017.
18 holes, length of course
5724m/6265 yds.
SSS 70 (par 71)
Charges: £20 daily.
For advance reservations
Tel: Motherwell 263017.
A practice area and catering
facilities are available.

Visitors are welcome by prior arrangement Monday to Friday. Secretary: Scott Connacher - Tel: Motherwell 265378 (after 5pm).

Muckhart
Clackmannanshire

Muckhart Golf Club
by Dollar.
Tel: Muckhart 781423.
18 holes, length of course 6034 yds.
SSS 70
Charges: £12.50 round (Mon-Fri), £18 (Sat/Sun), £18 daily (Mon-Fri), £24 (Sat/Sun).
Caddy cars and catering facilities are available.
Secretary: A.B. Robertson.
Professional: Mr. K. Salmoni.

Muirkirk
Ayrshire

Muirkirk Golf Club,
Furnace Road, Muirkirk.
9 holes, length of course 5350m (18 holes).
SSS 66
Charges: £5 daily. £20 weekly.
For advance reservations Tel: (0290) 61257.
A practice area and catering facilities are available.
Visitors are welcome all week.
Secretary: Mrs. M. Cassagranda
Tel: (0290) 61556.

Muir of Ord
Ross-shire

Muir of Ord Golf Club
Great North Road,
Muir of Ord IV6 7SX.
Tel: (0463) 870825.
18 holes, length of course 5129 yds.
SSS 65
Charges: April/Sept £12 daily (weekdays), £15 (Sat/Sun). Oct/March £10 daily (7 days).
Summer £50 weekly (Mon-Fri).
For advance reservations Tel: (0463) 871311/870825.
A practice area and catering facilities are available.
Visitors are welcome all week.
Administrator: Mrs. C. Moir
Tel: (0463) 870825.
Professional: Mr. G. Vivers
Tel: (0463) 871311.

Musselburgh
East Lothian

The Musselburgh Golf Club
Monktonhall, Musselburgh.
Tel: 031-665 2005/7055.
18 holes, length of course 6614 yds.
SSS 72.
Charges: On application.
Catering facilties are available except Tuesdays.
Visitors are welcome with reservation.
Secretary: S. Sullivan.
Professional: Mr. T. Stangoe.

Muthill
Perthshire

Muthill Golf Club
Peat Road, Muthill,
Crieff PH5 2AD.
(Further details on application).

Nairn

Nairn Golf Club
Seabank Road, Nairn.
Tel: (0667) 53208.
18 holes, length of course 6722 yds.
SSS 71
Par 72
Charges: £25 round (Mon-Fri), £30 (Sat/Sun); £35 daily (Mon-Fri), £40 (Sat/Sun).
For advance reservations Tel: (0667) 53208.
A practice area, caddies, caddy cars and catering facilities are available.
Visitors are welcome all week.
Secretary: Mr. J.G. Somerville - Tel: (0667) 53208.
Professional: Mr. R. Fyfe Tel: (0667) 52787.

Nairn Dunbar Golf Club
Lochloy Road,
Nairn IV12 5AE
Tel: (0667) 52741.
18 holes, length of course 6431 yds.
SSS 71
Charges: £15 per round, £20 daily (Mon-Fri). £20 per round, £25 daily (Sat/Sun).
A practice area and caddy cars are available.
Secretary: Mrs. S.J. MacLennan.
Professional: Brian Mason.

Nethy Bridge
Inverness-shire

Abernethy Golf Club
Tel: (0479) 821305.
(Further details on application).

Newburgh-on-Ythan
Aberdeenshire

Newburgh-on-Ythan Golf Club
51 Mavis Bank,
Newburgh, Ellon, AB4 0FB.
Tel: Newburgh 89438.
9 holes, length of course 6300 yds.
SSS 70
Charges: £10 daily (weekdays), £12 daily, (weekends).
For advance reservations Tel: Udny 2070 (Mr. J. Stewart - Match Sec.).
A practice area is available.
Visitors are welcome all week but club competitions every Tuesday evening.
Secretary: Mr. A.C. Stevenson - Tel: Newburgh 89438.

Newcastleton
Roxburghshire

Newcastleton Golf Club
Holm Hill,
Newcastleton.
9 holes, length of course 5748m
SSS 68
Charges: £6 per round/daily weekdays. £25 weekly.
For advance reservations Tel: (03873) 75257.
Visitors are welcome all week.
Secretary: F.J. Ewart
Tel: (03873) 75257.

New Cumnock
Ayrshire

New Cumnock Golf Club
(Further details on application).

New Galloway
Kirkcudbrightshire

New Galloway Golf Club
New Galloway,
Kirkcudbrightshire DG7 3RN.
9 holes, length of course 2313m/2529 yds.

SSS 65
Charges: £8 per day.
Visitors are welcome.
Secretary: Mr. A.R. Brown
Tel: (06443) 455.

Newmachar
Aberdeenshire

Newmachar Golf Club
Swailend, Newmachar
AB2 0UU.
Tel: (0651) 863002.
18 holes, length of course
6605 yds.
SSS 73
Charges: £16 Mon-Fri, £20 Sat
& Sun per round. £24 Mon-Fri,
£30 Sat & Sun daily.
For advance reservations
Tel: (0651) 863002.
Caddy cars and catering
facilities are available.
Visitors are welcome all week.
Secretary: George A. McIntosh
Tel: (0651) 863002.
Professional: Glenn Taylor
Tel: (0651) 862127.

Newton Mearns
Renfrewshire

**The East Renfrewshire
Golf Club**
Pilmuir.
Tel: Loganswell 258.
(Further details on application).

Eastwood Golf Club
Muirshield, Loganswell,
Newton Mearns,
Glasgow G77 6RX.
Tel: Loganswell 261.
18 holes, length of course
5886 yds.
SSS 68
Charges: £18 round, £26 daily.
(Subject to prior application and
approval).
For advance reservations
Tel: Loganswell 280.
Caddy cars and catering
facilities are available.
Visitors are welcome all week.
Secretary: C.B. Scouler
Tel: Loganswell 280 (a.m.
only).
Professional: S. Campbell
Tel: Loganswell 285.

Newtonmore
Inverness-shire

Newtonmore Golf Club
Tel: (0540) 673 328/878
Fax: (0540) 673 878.
Charges: £10 per round
midweek, £13 per round
weekends. £13 daily midweek,
£16 daily weekends (1993).
Secretary: R.J. Cheyne
Tel: (0540) 673878.
(Further details on application).

Newton Stewart
Wigtownshire

Newton Stewart Golf Club
Kirroughtree Avenue,
Minnigaff, Newton Stewart.
Tel: (0671) 2172.
18 holes, length of course
5588m/5970 yds.
SSS 69
Charges: £12 per round, £15
daily midweek. £15 per round,
£20 daily weekends and public
holidays.
For advance reservations
Tel: (0671) 2172.
Catering facilities are available.
Visitors are welcome all week.
Secretary: D.C. Matthewson
Tel: (0671) 3236.

North Berwick
East Lothian

*Glen Golf Club
East Links,
Tantallon Terrace,
North Berwick EH39 4LE.
Tel: (0620) 2221.
18 holes, length of course
6079 yds.
SSS 69
Charges: On application
Catering facilities available
during the season (Apr-Oct) and
at weekends throughout the
year.
Secretary: D.R. Montgomery -
Tel: Starter's box (0620) 2726.
Professional (shop only)
R. Affleck.

Oban
Argyll

Glencruitten Golf Course
Glencruitten Road, Oban.
Tel: (0631) 62868.
18 holes, length of course
4452 yds.
SSS 63
Charges: £9 round, £11 daily,
£45 weekly.
For advance reservations
Tel: (0631) 62868.
A practice area and catering
facilities are available.
Visitors are welcome Mon,
Tues, Wed, Fri and Suns.
Secretary: A.G. Brown
Tel: (0631) 64604 (after 6pm).

Old Meldrum
Aberdeenshire

Old Meldrum Golf Club
Kirk Brae, Old Meldrum.
Tel: (0651) 872648.
18 holes, length of course
5988 yds.
SSS 69 (Par 70) Medal Tees
SSS 66 (Par 68) Forward Tees
Charges: Per round/daily - £10
Mon-Fri, £15 Sat/Sun, weekly
(Mon-Fri) £35.
For reservations
Tel: (0651) 872648.
Visitors and visiting parties
welcome.
A practice area and bar facilities
are available.
Secretary: D. Petrie
Tel: (0651) 872383.

Paisley
Renfrewshire

Barshaw Golf Club
Barshaw Park, Paisley.
Tel: 041-889 2908.
18 holes, length of course
5703 yds.
SSS 67
Charges: £5.90 round; juniors/
OAP's/unemployed £3.
Visitors are welcome all week.
Secretary: Mr. W. Collins
Tel: 041-884 2533.

The Paisley Golf Club
Tel: 041-884 2292.
18 holes, length of course
5857m/6424 yds.
SSS 71
Charges: £16 round, £24 daily.

A practice area and catering facilities are available.
Secretary: W.J. Cunningham
Tel: 041-884 3903.
Professional: G.B. Gilmour
Tel: 041-554 4114.

Peebles
Peeblesshire

Peebles Golf Club
Kirkland Street, Peebles.
Tel: Peebles 20197.
18 holes, length of course
5612m/6137 yds.
SSS 69
Charges: On application.
A practice area, buggies, caddy cars and catering facilities are available.

Penicuik
Midlothian

Glencorse Golf Club
Milton Bridge,
Penicuik EH26 0RD.
Tel: Penicuik 676939.
18 holes, length of course
5205 yds.
SSS 66
Charges: £15 round, £20 daily. (Subject to review).
For advance reservations
Tel: Penicuik 677189 (Clubs/ Societies only).
Caddy cars and catering facilities are available.
Visitors are welcome on, Tues, Wed and Thurs.
Secretary: D.A. McNiven
Tel: Penicuik 677189.
Professional: Mr. C. Jones
Tel: Penicuik 676481.

Perth
Perthshire

The Craigie Hill Golf Club (1982) Ltd
Cherrybank, Perth.
18 holes, length of course
5379 yds.
SSS 66
Charges: £10 round (Mon-Fri), £15 daily (Mon-Fri), £20 daily (Sun).
For advance reservations
Tel: (0738) 22644.
A practice area, caddy cars and catering facilities are available.
Visitors are welcome all week except Saturdays.

Secretary: Mr. W.A. Miller
Tel: (0738) 20829.
Professional: Mr. F. Smith
Tel: (0738) 22644.

King James VI Golf Club
Moncreiffe Island, Perth.
Tel: Perth 25170/32460.
18 holes, length of course
5177m/5664 yds.
SSS 68
Charges: £13 round, £20 daily (Mon-Fri), £27 (Sun) (1993).
For advance reservations
Tel: Perth 32460.
A practice area, caddy cars and catering facilities are available.

Murrayshall Golf Club,
Murrayshall Country House Hotel & Golf Course,
Scone, Perthshire PH2 7PH.
Tel: (0738) 51171.
18 holes, length of course
5901m/6460 yds.
SSS 71
Charges: On Application
For advance reservations
Tel: (0738) 51171.
Caddies, caddy cars, buggies, practice area and catering facilities are available.
Visitors are welcome all week.
Professional: Neil MacIntosh
Tel: (0738) 52784.

North Inch Golf Club,
North Inch (off Hay Street), Perth.
18 holes, length of course
5178m.
SSS 65
Charges: £4.60 Mon-Fri, £6.20 Sat & Sun per round.
For advance reservations
Tel: (0738) 36481.
Catering facilities are available.
Visitors are welcome all week.

Peterhead
Aberdeenshire

Craigewan Golf Course
Peterhead Golf Club
Craigewan Links,
Peterhead.
Tel: (0779) 72149.
18 holes, length of course
6173 yds.
SSS 70
Charges £12 weekdays, £16 Sat & Sun daily.
A practice area and limited catering facilities are available.

Visitors are welcome all week - restricted on Saturdays.
Secretary: W. Bradford
Tel: (0779) 72149.

Pitlochry
Perthshire

Pitlochry Golf Course Ltd.,
Pitlochry.
Tel: Pitlochry 2792 (bookings).
18 holes, length of course
5811 yds.
SSS 68.
Charges: (Weekday day tickets, 1st Apr to 31st Oct): Adult £13, Junior £3. (Saturday day tickets, 1st Apr to 31st Oct) Adult £16, Junior £5. (Sunday day tickets, 1st Apr to 31st Oct) Adult/ Junior £16. Restricted course: (1st Nov to 31st Mar) day ticket, any day: Adult £6, Junior £1.50.
Caddy cars, tuition and catering facilities are available.
Visitors are welcome all week.
Secretary: D.M. McKenzie.
Professional: George Hampton
Tel: Pitlochry 2792.

Port Glasgow
Renfrewshire

Port Glasgow Golf Club
Devol Road, Port Glasgow.
Tel: (0475) 704181.
18 holes, length of course
5592m/5712 yds.
SSS 68
Charges: £12 round, £18 daily.
Weekly by arrangement.
For advance reservations
Tel: (0475) 704181.
A practice area and catering facilities are available.
Visitors are welcome uninvited before 3.55 pm, not on Saturdays and invited only Sundays.
Secretary: N.L. Mitchell
Tel: (0475) 706273.

Portlethen
Aberdeenshire

Portlethen Golf Club
Badentoy Road,
Portlethen AB1 4TU.
Tel: (0221) 782575.
18 holes, length of course
6707 yds.
SSS 72
Charges £10 weekdays, £15

weekends per round. £15
weekdays (only) daily.
For advance reservations Tel:
(0221) 782575.
Caddy cars, practice area and
catering facilities are available.
Visitors are welcome Mon-Fri;
weekend with member.
Secretary: Mr. C. Harris
Tel: (0221) 782575.
Professional: Muriel Thomson
Tel: (0221) 782571.

Portmahomack
Ross-shire

Tarbat Golf Club
Portmahomack.
Tel: (0862) 87 236.
(Further details on application).

Portpatrick
Wigtownshire

Portpatrick Golf Club
Tel: (0776) 81 273.
18 holes Dunskey Course, 9
holes Dinvin Course.
Charges: Dunskey - £13 round,
£20 daily (Mon-Fri), £16 round,
£24 daily (Sat/Sun). £65
weekly. Dinvin - £5 (18 holes),
£10 daily. Juniors under 18 half
stated price.
Secretary: J.A. Horberry
Tel: (0776) 81273

Port William
Wigtownshire

St. Medan Golf Club
Monreith, Port William.
Tel: Port William 358.
9 holes, length of course
2277 yds.
SSS 62
Charges: £10 round/daily. £40
weekly.
Catering facilities are available.
Visitors are welcome all week.
Secretary: D. O'Neill
Tel: Whithorn 555.

Prestonpans
East Lothian

**Royal Musselburgh Golf
Club**
Preston Grange House,
Prestonpans.
Tel: (0875) 810276.
18 holes, length of course

6255 yds.
SSS 70
Charges: £16.50 (round)
weekdays, £27.50 (daily).
£27.50 (round) weekends
(1993).
Advance reservations in writing
preferable.
Caddy cars, practice area and
catering facilities are available.
Visitors are welcome weekdays,
except Friday afternoons.
Secretary: T.H. Hardie
Tel: (0875) 810276.
Professional: J. Henderson Tel:
(0875) 810139.

Prestwick
Ayrshire

Prestwick Golf Club
2 Links Road, Prestwick.
Tel: (0292) 77404.
18 holes, length of course
6544 yds.
SSS 72
Charges: On application.
Caddies, caddy cars, practice
area and catering facilities are
available.
Visitors are welcome Mon,
Tues, Wed, Fri 8-9 am, 10 am-
12.30 pm and 2.45-4.00 pm
Thursday 8-11 am.
Secretary: D.E. Donaldson.
Professional: F.C. Rennie.

**Prestwick
St. Cuthbert Golf Club**
East Road,
Prestwick KA9 2SX.
Tel: (0292) 77101.
18 holes, length of course
6470 yds.
SSS 71
Charges: £18 round, £24 daily.
For advance reservations
Tel: (0292) 77101.
Catering facilities (except
Thursdays) are available.
Visitors are welcome Monday
to Friday (not on weekends or
public holidays).
Secretary: R.Morton
Tel: (0292) 77101.

**Prestwick
St. Nicholas Golf Club**
Grangemuir Road,
Prestwick KA9 1SN.
Tel: (0292) 77608.
18 holes, length of course
5441m/5952 yds.

SSS 69
Charges: £18 round (after 2
pm), £30 daily.
For advance reservations
Tel: (0292) 77608.
Caddy cars and catering
facilities are available.
Visitors are welcome Monday
to Friday only.
Secretary: J.R. Leishman
Tel: (0292) 77608.
Professional: S. Smith
Tel: (0292) 79755.

Pumpherston
West Lothian

Pumpherston Golf Club
Drumshoreland Road,
Pumpherston,
Livingston EH53 0LF.
Tel: (0506) 32869.
9 holes, length of course
4712m/5154 yds.
SSS 65
Restricted practice area and
catering facilities are available.
Visitors are welcome all week,
only with a member.
Secretary: A.H. Docharty
Tel: (0506) 854652.

Reay
By Thurso, Caithness

Reay Golf Club
Tel: Reay 288.
18 holes, length of course
5372m/5876 yds.
SSS 68
Charges: £10 round/daily, £30
weekly.
A practice area is available.
Secretary: Miss P. Peebles
Tel: Reay 537.

Renfrew
Renfrewshire

Renfrew Golf Club
Blythswood Estate,
Inchinnan Road, Renfrew.
Tel: 041-886 6692.
18 holes, length of course
6231m/6818 yds.
SSS 73
Charges: £16 round, £25 daily.
Catering services are available.
Secretary: A.D. Brockie ·
Tel: 041-886 6692.

Rigside
Lanarkshire

Douglas Water Golf Club
Ayr Road, Rigside.
9 holes, length of course
2945m
SSS 69
Charges: £5 (Mon-Fri) daily, £7
Sat/Sun.
Please write for advance
reservations.
A practice area is available,
light refreshments are available
at the weekend.
Visitors are welcome all week -
restrictions on Saturdays due to
competition.
Secretary: Mr.R. McMillan.

Rothesay
Isle of Bute

Port Bannatyne Golf Club
Bannatyne Mains Road,
Port Bannatyne.
Tel: (0700) 502009.
13 holes, length of course
4256m/4654 yds.
SSS 63
Charges: £7.50 daily, including
weekends. £30 weekly.
For advance reservations
Tel: (0700) 502009.
Visitors are welcome all week.
Secretary: Mr. I.L. MacLeod
Tel: (0700) 502009.

Rothesay Golf Club
Canada Hill,
Rothesay, Isle of Bute.
Tel: Clubhouse (0700) 502244.
18 holes, length of course
5370 yds.
Charges: On Application (day
tickets only).
Pre-booking essential for
Saturday/Sunday.
Catering facilities available.
Secretary: J. Barker
Tel: (0700) 503744.
Professional: J. Dougal
Tel: (0700) 503554.

Rutherglen
Lanarkshire

Blairbeth Golf Club
Fernhill, Rutherglen.
Tel: 041-634 3355.
(Further details on application).

Cathkin Braes Golf Club
Cathkin Road,
Rutherglen, Glasgow G73 4SE.
Tel: 041-634 6605.
18 holes, length of course
6208 yds.
SSS 71
Charges: £16 per round. £25
daily.
For advance reservations
Tel: 041-634 0650.
Caddy cars, practice area and
catering facilities are available.
Visitors are welcome Mon to
Fri.
Secretary: G.L. Stevenson
Tel: 041-634 6605.
Professional: S. Bree
Tel: 041-634 0650.

St. Andrews
Fife

Royal & Ancient Golf Club
Tel: St. Andrews 72112/3.
(Further details on application).

**St. Andrews Balgove
Course**
9 holes beginners' course. 18
holes.
Charges: £5 per round.
Visitors are welcome.
Golf Manager: John Lindsey ·
Tel: St. Andrews 75757.

St. Andrews Eden Course
18 holes, length of course
5588m/6112 yds.
SSS 70
Charges: £16 round, all week:
£100 7 day ticket (unlimited
play).
For advance reservations
Tel: St. Andrews 74269.
Caddies are available.
Golf Manager: John Lindsey
Tel: St. Andrews 75757.

**St. Andrews Jubilee
Course**
18 holes, length of course
6223m/7805 yds.
SSS 73
Charges: £16 round, all week:
£100 7 day ticket (unlimited
play).
For advance reservations
Tel: St. Andrews 75757.
Caddies and caddy cars
available.
Golf Manager: John Lindsey
Tel: St. Andrews 75757.

St. Andrews New Course
18 holes, length of course

6039m/6604 yds.
SSS 71
Charges: £18 round, all week:
£100 7 day ticket (unlimited
play).
For advance reservations
Tel: St. Andrews 75757.
Caddies and caddy cars are
available.
Golf Manager: John Lindsey
Tel: St. Andrews 75757.

St. Andrews Old Course
18 holes, length of course
6004m/6566 yds.
SSS 72
Charges: £40 round all week
(closed Sunday).
For advance reservations
Tel: St. Andrews 73393.
Caddies are available.
A Handicap Certificate or letter
of introduction is required from
visitors.
Golf Manager: John Lindsey
Tel: St. Andrews 75757.

Strathtyrum Course
18 holes, length of course
4661m/5094 yds.
SSS 65
Charges: £12 per round.
Visitors are welcome.
Golf Manager: John Lindsey
Tel: St. Andrews 75757.

St. Boswells
Roxburghshire

St. Boswells Golf Club
St. Boswells, Roxburghshire.
Tel: (0835) 22359.
9 holes, length of course
5250 yds.
SSS 65
Charges: Mon-Sun £10.
For advance reservations
Tel: (0835) 22359.
Visitors are welcome all week.
Secretary: G.B. Ovens
Tel: (0835) 22359.

St. Fillans
Perthshire

St. Fillans Golf Club
South Lochearn Road,
St. Fillans.
Tel: St. Fillans 312.
9 holes, length of course
4812m/5628 yds.
SSS 68
Charges: £8 round, £12 day

ticket (Mon-Fri); £10 round, £14 day ticket (Sat/Sun). Caddy cars and limited catering facilities are available. Visitors are welcome all week. Visiting clubs by arrangement. Secretary: J. Allison Tel: Comrie 70951.

Saline
Fife

Saline Golf Club
Kinneddar Hill,
Saline, Fife.
Tel: (0383) 852 591.
9 holes, length of course
5302 yds.
SSS 66
Charges: £8 weekdays, £10 weekends.
For advance reservations
Tel: Clubhouse (0383) 852 591.
Practice area. Catering facilities are available by prior arrangement.
Visitors are welcome all week, except Saturdays.
Secretary: R. Hutchison
Tel: (0383) 852 344.

Sanquhar
Dumfriesshire

Euchan Golf Course
Sanquhar.
Tel: (0659) 50577.
9 holes, length of course
5144m.
SSS 68
Charges: £6 round, £8 daily
(Mon-Fri), £10 (Sat/Sun).
For advance reservations
Tel: (0659) 58181.
Catering facilities (advance notice by parties) are available.
Visitors are welcome all week.
Secretary: Mrs. J. Murray
Tel: (0659) 58181.

Scarinish
Isle of Tiree

Vaul Golf Club
9 holes, length of course
2911 yds.
SSS 70 (18 holes)
Secretary: N.J. MacArthur
Tel: (08792) 339.
(Further details on application).

Sconser
Isle of Skye

Isle of Skye Golf Club
(Formerly Sconser Golf Club)
Sconser, Isle of Skye.
9 holes, length of course
4385m/4798 yds.
SSS 63
Charges: £7 round, £20 weekly;
£14 per 3-days.
Visitors are welcome all week.
Advance reservations are only required for large parties
Tel: Secretary · (0478) 2277.
Secretary: J. Stephen
Tel: (0478) 2000.

Skeabost Bridge
Isle of Skye

Skeabost Golf Club
Skeabost House Hotel,
Skeabost Bridge,
Isle of Skye IV51 9NP.
Tel: 047-032-215
9 holes, length of course
1597 yds.
SSS 29
Charges: £6 per daily.
For advanced reservations
Tel: 047-032-215
Catering facilities are available.
Visitors are welcome all week.
Secretary: John Stuart
Tel: 047 032 322.

Selkirk
Selkirkshire

Selkirk Golf Club
Selkirk Hills, Selkirk.
Tel: (0750) 20621.
9 holes, length of course
5636 yds.
Charges: £8 daily.
Visitors are welcome without reservation.
Secretary: R. Davies
Tel: (0750) 20427.

Shotts
Lanarkshire

Blairhead Golf Course
Shotts Golf Club
Blairhead, Shotts.
Tel: Shotts 820431.
Charges: day ticket £14.
Visitors are welcome weekdays.
(Further details on application).

Skelmorlie
Ayrshire

Skelmorlie Golf Course
Belthglass Road,
Upper Skelmorlie, Ayrshire.
Tel: Wemyss Bay 520152O.
13 holes, length of course 5056m.
SSS 65
Charges: Mon-Fri (round) £9;
(daily) £12. Sat/Sun (round) £10;
(daily) £15. Weekly (5-days) £30.
2 weeks (10 days) £50.
Catering facilities are available for visitors and parties.
Visitors are welcome all week, except Saturdays.
Secretary: Mrs. A. Fahey
Tel: 0475 520774.

Southend
Argyll

Dunaverty Golf Club
Southend,
by Campbeltown, Argyll.
Tel: (0586) 83 677.
18 holes, length of course
4799 yds.
SSS 64
Charges: £7 round, £10 daily, £30 weekly.
For advance reservations
Tel: (0586) 83 698/677.
Catering facilities are available.
Visitors are welcome all week without reservation, but check for club competitions.
Secretary: J. Galbraith
Tel: (0586) 83 698.

Southerness
Kirkcudbrightshire

Southerness Golf Club
Southerness,
Dumfries DG2 8AZ.
Tel: (0387) 88 677.
18 holes, length of course
6564 yds.
SSS 72
Charges: £23 (Mon-Fri) daily, £30 (weekend). £92 weekly (Mon-Fri).
For advance reservations
Tel: (0387) 88 677.
A practice area, caddy cars and catering facilities are available.
Visitors - members of recognised golf clubs only are welcome all week.
Secretary: W.D. Ramage
Tel: (0387) 88 677.

South Queensferry
West Lothian

Dundas Parks Golf Club
Hope Cottage,
Loch Road,
South Queensferry EH30 9LS.
Tel: 031-331 1416.
9 holes, length of course
6024 yds.
SSS 69
Charges £8.00 per round/daily.
For advance reservations
Tel: 031-331 1416.
A practice area is available.
Visitors are welcome by prior
arrangement with secretary.
Secretary: Keith D. Love
Tel: 031-331 1416.

South Uist
Western Isles

Links-Land Golf Course
Askernish Golf Club
Askernish.
Tel: Lochboisdale 541.
(Further details on application).

Spean Bridge
Inverness-shire

Spean Bridge Golf Club
Spean Bridge,
Inverness-shire
Tel: (0397) 703379.
9 holes, length of course
2203 yds.
SSS 62
Charges: £7 per day (18 holes).
Visitors are welcome all week
(except Tuesdays after 5pm).
Secretary: John Lennan
Tel: (0397) 703379.

Spey Bay
Morayshire

Spey Bay Golf Club
Spey Bay Hotel, Spey Bay,
Fochabers IV32 7JP.
Tel: (0343) 820424.
18 holes, length of course
6059 yds.
SSS 69
Charges: Mon-Sat £5.50 per
round, Sun £7 per round.
Caddy cars, practice area and
catering facilities available at
the hotel.
Visitors and golf outings
welcome.
(Enquiries to hotel manager).

Stevenston
Ayrshire

Ardeer Golf Club
Greenhead, Stevenston.
Tel: (0294) 64542.
18 holes, length of course
6630 yds.
SSS 72
Charges: £10 (Mon-Fri), £12
(Sun), round; £18 (Mon-Fri),
£24 (Sun) daily.
For advance reservations Tel:
(0294) 65316/64542 (secretary).
Caddy cars, practice area and
catering facilities are available.
Visitors are welcome all week,
except Saturdays.
Secretary: T. Cumming
Tel: (0294) 56633.
Starter/Shop: R. Rodgers
Tel: (0294) 601327.

Stirling
Stirlingshire

Stirling Golf Club
Queen's Road,
Stirling FK8 3AA.
Tel: Stirling 473801.
18 holes, length of course
6409 yds.
SSS Medal 71, Front Tee 69.
Charges: £17 round, £23 daily.
A practice area, caddy cars and
catering facilities are available.
Visitors are welcome by
arrangement.
Secretary: Mr. W.C. McArthur
Tel: Stirling 464098/461348.
Professional: Mr. I. Collins Tel:
Stirling 471490.

Stonehaven
Kincardineshire

Stonehaven Golf Club
Cowie, Stonehaven AB3 2RH.
Tel: (0569) 62124.
18 holes, length of course
4669m/5103 yds.
SSS 65
Charges: £13 daily (Mon-Fri),
£18 (Sat/Sun), £50 weekly,
£70 fortnightly.
For advance reservations
Tel: (0569) 62124.
A practice area, catering & full
licensing facilities are available.
Visitors are welcome Monday
to Friday. Late afternoon and
evening on Saturday and
Sunday.

Secretary: Mr. R.O. Blair
Tel: (0569) 62124.

Stornoway
Isle of Lewis

Stornoway Golf Course
Tel: Stornoway 2240.
(Further details on application).

Stranraer
Wigtownshire

*Stranraer Golf Club
Creachmore, By Stranraer.
Tel: Leswalt 245.
18 holes, length of course
5760m/6308 yds.
SSS 71
Charges: £15 round (Mon-Fri),
£20 round (Sat/Sun), £20 daily
(Mon-Fri), £25 daily (Sat/Sun).
A practice area, caddy cars and
catering facilities are available.
Secretary: Mr. W.I. Wilson
Tel: Stranraer 3539.

Strathaven
Lanarkshire

Strathaven Golf Club
Overton Avenue,
Glasgow Road, Strathaven.
Tel: Strathaven 20421.
18 holes, length of course
5696m/6226 yds.
SSS 70
Charges: £17 round, £24 daily.
For advance reservations Tel:
Strathaven 20421.
A practice area, caddy cars and
catering facilities are available.
Secretary: Mr. A.W. Wallace
Tel: Strathaven 20421.
Professional: Mr. M. McCrorie
Tel: Strathaven 21812.

Strathpeffer
Ross-shire

Strathpeffer Spa Golf Club
Strathpeffer IV14 9AS.
Tel: (0997) 421219.
18 holes, length of course
4000m/4792 yds.
SSS 65
Charges: Weekdays - £10
round,£15 daily; (Sat/Sun) £12
round, £18 daily.
For advance reservations
Tel: (0997) 421219.
A practice area, caddy cars and
catering facilities are available.

Visitors are welcome all week.
Secretary: Mr. N. Roxburgh -
Tel: (0997) 421396.

Strathtay
by Aberfeldy, Perthshire

Strathtay Golf Club
Tel: Strathtay 367.
9 holes, length of course
4082 yds (18 holes).
SSS 63
Charges: £8 (weekdays) daily,
juniors £2; £10 Sats/Suns,
juniors £3. £25 weekly tickets
(5 days).
For advance reservations
Tel: Strathtay 367.
Visitors are welcome all week,
except Sun 12-5 and Mon 6-9.
Secretary: J. Armstrong·Payne ·
(All Correspondence ·
Tighanoisinn, Grandtully, By
Aberfeldy, PH15 2QT)
Tel: Strathtay 367.

Stromness
Orkney

Stromness Golf Club
Ness, Stromness.
Tel: Stromness 850593.
(Further details on application).

Tain
Ross-shire

Tain Golf Club
Tain, Ross-shire.
Tel: (0862) 892314.
Length of course 6238 yds.
SSS 70
Charges: £12 round, £18 daily
(Mon-Fri); £18 round, £24 daily
(Sat/Sun).
For advance reservations
Tel: (0862) 892314.
Full catering facilities are
available.
Visitors are welcome.
Secretary: Mrs. K.D. Ross.

Tarbert
Argyllshire

Tarbert Golf Club
Kilberry Road, Tarbert.
Tel: (0880) 820565.
9 holes, length of course
4744 yds.
SSS 64
Charges: £5 (9 holes), £8 (18

holes). £10 daily. £30 weekly.
Licensed clubhouse available.
Visitors are welcome without
reservation.
Secretary: Peter Cupples
Tel: (0880) 820536.

Tarland
Aberdeenshire

Tarland Golf Club
Aberdeen Road, Tarland.
Tel: (03398) 81413.
9 holes, length of course
5386m/5888 yds.
SSS 68 (18 holes)
Charges: £10 (Mon-Fri), £12
(Sat-Sun), £40 weekly, £70
fortnightly.
For advance reservations
Tel: (03398) 81413 (no
reservations at weekends).
Caddy cars and practice area are
available.
Visitors are welcome all week,
but advise 'phoning regarding
weekends.
Secretary: J.H. Honeyman
Tel: (0224) 323111.

Taynuilt
Argyll

Taynuilt Golf Club
Laroch, Taynuilt.
9 holes, length of course
3674 yds.
SSS 61
Charges: £5.00 per round/daily.
Visitors are welcome all week.
Secretary: Mairead MacLeod
Tel: (086 62) 429.

Tayport
Fife

Scotscraig Golf Club
Golf Road, Tayport DD6 9DZ.
Tel: (0382) 552515.
18 holes, length of course
6496 yds.
SSS 71
Charges: On application.
Caddies by arrangement, caddy
cars, practice area and catering
facilities are available.
Visitors are welcome on
weekdays, or on weekends by
prior arrangement.
Secretary: K. Gourlay.

Thornhill
Dumfriesshire

Thornhill Golf Club
Thornhill.
Tel: (0848) 330546.
18 holes, length of course
6011 yds.
SSS 69
Par 71
Charges: £16 weekdays, £20
weekends.
For advance reservations Tel:
(0848) 330546 (Club Steward).
A practice area and catering
facilities are available.
Visitors are welcome all week.
Secretary: R.L. Ken.

Thornton
Fife

Thornton Golf Club
Station Road,
Thornton, KY1 4DW.
Tel: (0592) 771111.
18 holes, length of course
5560m/6177 yds.
SSS 69
Charges: £12 weekdays, £18
weekends per round; £18
weekdays, £27 weekends daily.
Juniors 50% off adult rate.
For advance reservations
Tel: (0592) 771111.
Practice area and catering
facilities are available.
Visitors are welcome all week.
Secretary: Neil Robertson
Tel: (0592) 771111.

Thurso
Caithness

Thurso Golf Club
Newlands of Geise, Thurso.
Tel: Thurso 63807.
(Further details on application).

Tighnabruaich
Argyllshire

Kyles of Bute Golf Club
Copeswood,
Tighnabruaich PA21 2BE.
Tel: (0700) 811 601.
9 holes, length of course
2389 yds.
SSS 64
Charges: £5 daily.
Secretary: Mr. J.A. Carruthers.

Tillicoultry
Clackmannanshire

Tillicoultry Golf Course
Alva Road, Tillicoultry.
9 holes, length of course
4518m/5266 yds.
SSS 66
Charges: £8 round Mon-Fri (18
holes), £11 after 4pm. Sat-Sun
£13.50 round.
For advance reservations
Tel: (0259) 50124.
A practice area and catering
facilities are available.
Visitors are welcome all week
(except competition days).
Secretary: Mr. R. Whitehead
Tel: (0259) 50124.

Tobermory
Isle of Mull

Tobermory Golf Club
Tobermory.
9 holes, length of course
4474m/4921 yds.
SSS 64
Charges: £9 daily, juniors £4;
£30 weekly, juniors £15.
For advance reservations
Tel: (0688) 2020.
Visitors are welcome.
Secretary: Dr. W.H. Clegg
Tel: (0688) 2013.

Torphins
Aberdeenshire

Torphins Golf Club
Tel: (03398) 82115.
9 holes, length of course
4660 yds.
SSS 63
Charges: £10 daily. £12
weekends.
Members evening from 5pm
Tuesdays.
Secretary: Mrs. Sue Mortimer
Tel: (03398) 82563.

Troon
Ayrshire

*Darley Golf Course
Harling Drive,
Troon, KA10 6NF
c/o Kyle & Carrick
District Council,
30 Miller Road, Ayr.
Tel: (0292) 312464.
18 holes, length of course
6327 yds.

SSS 70
Charges: £12.00 round; £18.00
daily ticket; 5-day tickets
£50.00.
Postal bookings only.
A practice area, caddy cars and
catering facilities are available.
Visitors are welcome all week.
Secretary: Starters Office
Tel: (0292) 312464.
Professional: Gordon McKinlay
Tel: (0292) 312464.

*Fullarton Golf Course
St Meddans Golf Club
Harling Drive,
Troon KA10 6NF.
c/o Kyle and Carrick
District Council,
30 Miller Road, Ayr.
Tel: (0292) 312464.
18 holes, length of course
4784 yds.
SSS 63
Charges: £8.00 per round;
£14.00 daily ticket; 5-day ticket
£50.00.
Postal bookings only.
A practice area, caddy cars and
catering facilities are available.
Visitors are welcome all week.
Secretary: Starters Office
Tel: (0292) 312464.
Professional: Gordon McKinlay
Tel: (0292) 312464.

Lochgreen Golf Course
Harling Drive,
Troon KA10 6NF
c/o Kyle & Carrick
District Council,
30 Miller Road, Ayr.
Tel: (0292) 312464.
18 holes, length of course
6765 yds.
SSS 72
Charges: £4.80 round
(Mon-Fri), £5.80 (Sat/Sun),
£7.60 daily (Mon-Fri), £9.20
(Sat/Sun), £28.40 weekly.
Postal bookings only.
A practice area, caddy cars and
catering facilities are available.
Visitors are welcome all week.
Secretary: Starters Office
Tel: (0292) 312464.
Professional: Gordon McKinlay
Tel: (0292) 312464.

Royal Troon Golf Club
Old Course,
Craigend Road, Troon
KA10 6LD.
Tel: (0292) 311555.
18 holes, length of course

7097 yds.
SSS 74
Charges: £75 daily inc. lunch
(includes 1 round on both
courses). (No ladies or under-
18's).
Caddies and catering facilities
(please advise 1 week before-
hand) are available
Visitors are welcome Mon, Tues
and Thurs only with advance
reservations.
Secretary: J.D. Montgomerie.
Professional: R. Brian
Anderson.

Royal Troon Golf Club
Portland Course,
Crosbie Road,
Troon KA10 6EP.
Tel: (0292) 311555.
18 holes, length of course
6274 yds.
SSS 71
Charges: £45 daily inc. lunch
(composite fee).
Catering facilities are available
Visitors are welcome Mon, Tues
and Thurs only with advance
reservations.
Secretary: J.D. Montgomerie.
Professional: R. Brian
Anderson.

Turnberry
Ayrshire

Ailsa & Arran
Turnberry Hotel & Golf
Courses & Spa
Tel: (0655) 31000.
2 x 18 holes, length of course
Ailsa 6408 yds., Arran
6276 yds.
SSS Ailsa 72, Arran 70.
A practice area, caddies, trolleys
and catering facilities are
available.
Clubhouse Manager: Mr. E.C.
Bowman
Professional: Mr. R.S. Jamieson

Turriff
Aberdeenshire

Turriff Golf Club
Rosehall, Turriff.
Tel: (0888) 62982.
18 holes, length of course
6145 yds.
SSS 69
Charges: £10 round (Mon-Fri)
£13 (Sat/Sun); £13 daily (Mon-
Fri), £16 (Sat/Sun).

For advance reservations Tel: (0888) 63025.
A small practice area, clubs, caddy cars and catering facilities are available. Visitors are welcome all week and after 10 am Sat/Sun.
Secretary: Mr. J.D. Stott
Tel: (0888) 62982.
Professional: Mr. R. Smith
Tel: (0888) 63025.

Uddingston
Lanarkshire

Calderbraes Golf Club
57 Roundknowe Road,
Uddingston.
Tel: Uddingston 813425.
(Further details on application).

Uphall
West Lothian

Uphall Golf Club
Tel: 0506 856404.
(Further details on application).

West Calder
West Lothian

Harburn Golf Club
West Calder EH55 8RS.
Tel: (0506) 871256.
18 holes, length of course 5340m/5843 yds.
SSS 68
Charges: £12.50 (Mon-Fri), £18.50 (Sat/Sun) round; £18.50 (Mon-Fri), £25 (Sat/Sun) daily.
For advance reservations
Tel: (0506) 871256.
Caddy cars, practice area and catering facilities are available. Visitors are welcome all week.
Secretary: F. Vinter
Tel: (0506) 871131.
Professional: S. Crookston
Tel: (0506) 871582.

West Kilbride
Ayrshire

West Kilbride Golf Club
Fullerton Drive,
West Kilbride KA23 9HT.
Tel: (0294) 823128.
18 holes, length of course 6247 yds.
SSS 70
Charges: On Application.
For advance reservations
Tel: (0294) 823042.

A practice area, caddy cars and catering facilities are available. Visitors are welcome Monday to Friday.
Secretary: E.D. Jefferies
Tel: (0294) 823911.
Professional: G. Howie
Tel: (0294) 823042.

West Linton
Peeblesshire

West Linton Golf Club
West Linton.
Tel: (0968) 60463.
18 holes, length of course 5607m/6132 yds.
SSS 69
Charges: £14 round (Mon-Fri), £22 (Sat/Sun), £20 daily (Mon-Fri).
For advance reservations
Tel: (0968) 60256.
A practice area and catering facilities are available.
Visiting parties welcome Mon-Fri, casual visitors welcome also, at weekend after 1pm.
Secretary: G. Scott
Tel: (0968) 60970 (Office), (0968) 75843 (Home).

Westray
Orkney

Westray Golf Club
(Further details on application).

Whalsay
Shetland Isles

Whalsay Golf Club
Skaw Taing, Whalsay.
18 holes, length of course 6009 yds.
Charges: Daily £5. Weekly £20. With member £2.
A practice area is available.
Visitors are welcome all week.
Joint Secretaries: H. Sandison & C. Hutchison
Tel: (08066) 450.

Whitburn
West Lothian

*Polkemmet Country Park Golf Club
West Lothian District Council,
Park Centre, Whitburn
EH47 0AD.
Tel: (0501) 43905.

9 holes, length of course 2969m.
Charges: On application
Caddy cars, practice area and catering facilities are available. Visitors are welcome all week.

Whiting Bay
Isle of Arran

Whiting Bay Golf Club
Tel: (07707) 487.
(Further details on application).

Wick
Caithness

Wick Golf Club
Reiss,
Caithness KW1 4RW.
Tel: (0955) 2726.
18 holes, length of course 5976 yds.
SSS 69
Charges: Weekdays £10 daily; weekends £12 daily; weekly £40; juniors £3; fortnightly £50.
Visitors welcome without reservations.
Society meetings catered for.
Secretary:
Mrs. M.S.W. Abernethy
Tel: (0955) 2702.

Wigtown
Wigtownshire

Wigtown & Bladnoch Golf Club
Wigtown, Newton Stewart.
Tel: (098 84) 3354.
9 holes, length of course 2521m.
SSS 67
Charges: £7 daily weekdays; £10 round Sat/Suns.
Visitors are welcome all week.
Secretary: L. Duxbury
Tel: (098 84) 2473.

Wishaw
Lanarkshire

Wishaw Golf Club
55 Cleland Road, Wishaw.
Tel: Wishaw 372869.
18 holes, length of course 6073 yds.
SSS 69
Charges: £20 daily; midweek per round £12. £25 (Sun).
A practice area, caddy cars and catering facilities are available.
Secretary: D.D. Gallacher.
Professional: J. Campbell.

Notes

MAPS

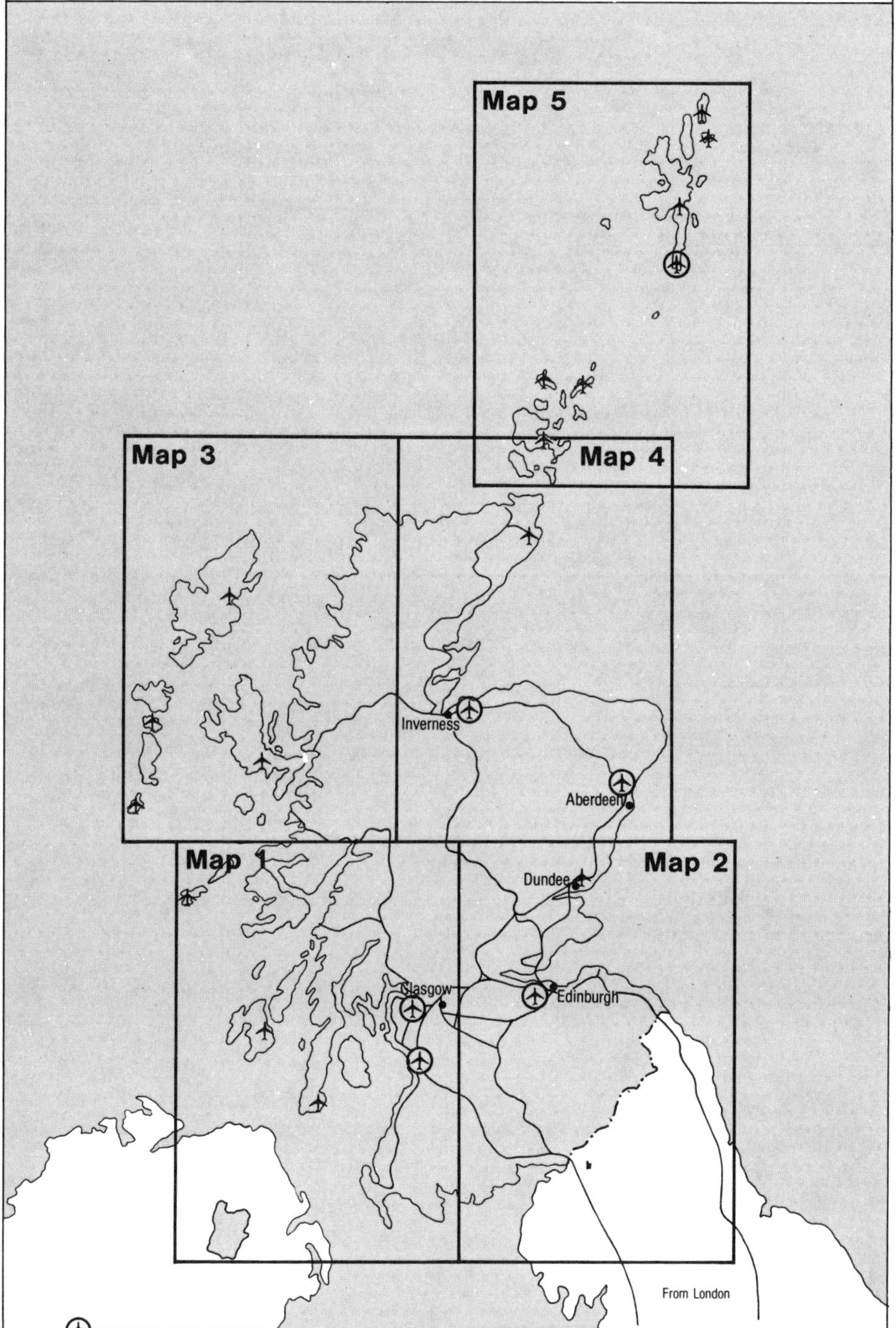

Map 5

Map 3

Map 4

Inverness

Aberdeen

Map 1

Map 2

Dundee

Glasgow

Edinburgh

From London

✈ MAJOR AIRPORTS —— RAILWAY ROUTES © Baynefield Carto-Graphics Ltd 1991

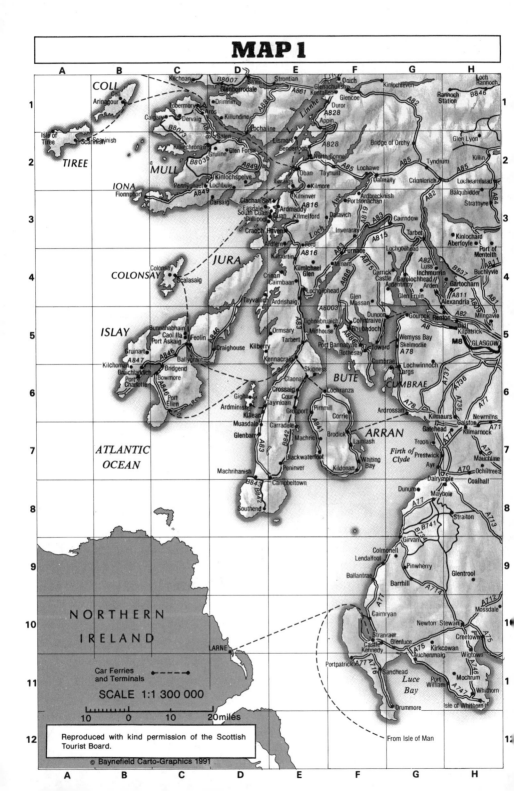

MAP 2

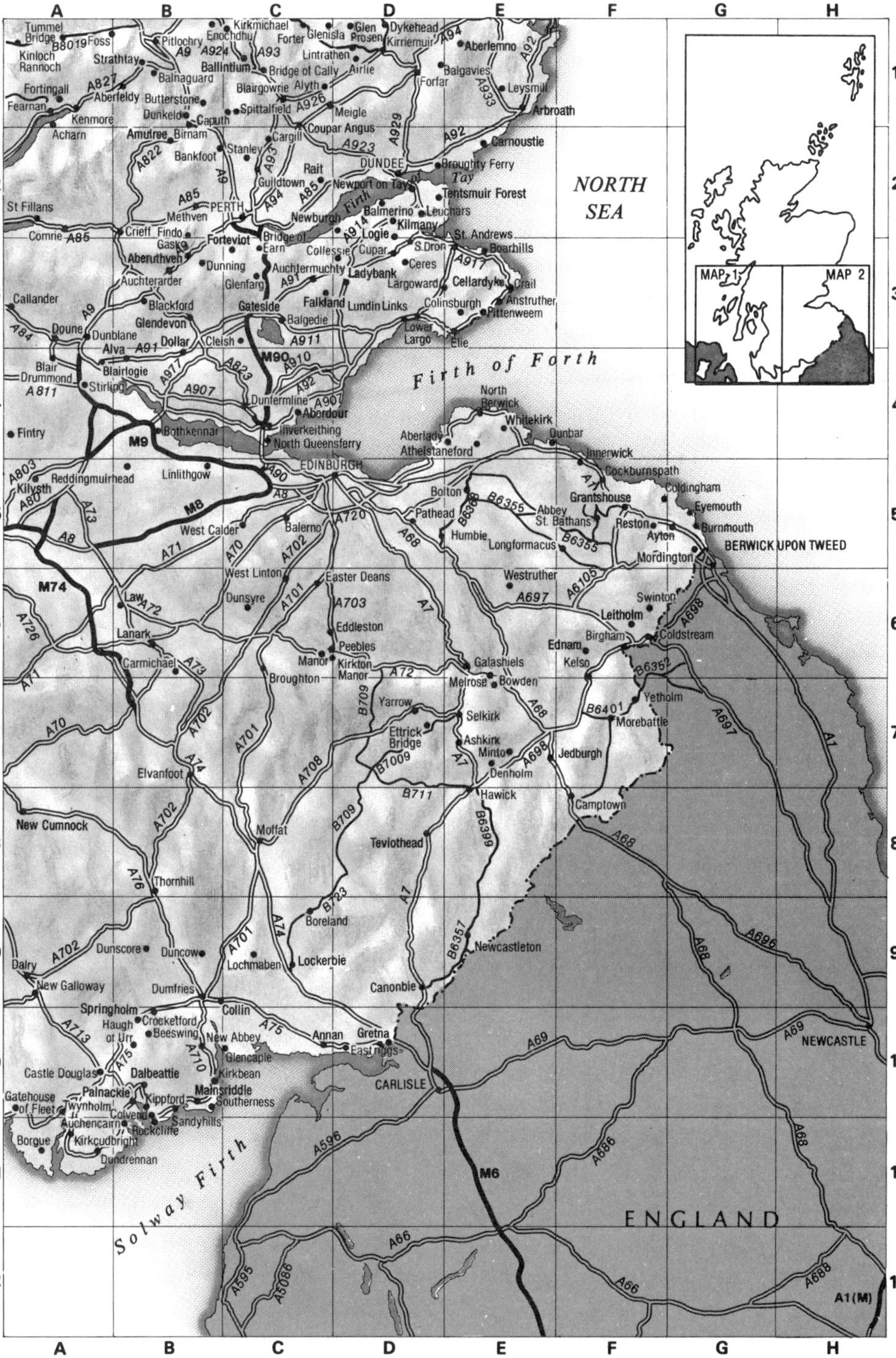

A B C D E F G H

NORTH
SEA

MAP 1 MAP 2

Tummel Bridge B8019 Foss Kirkmichael Glen Dykehead
Pitlochry Enochdhu Forter Glenisla Prosen Kirriemuir A94
Kinloch A9 A924 A93 Lintrathen Aberlemno A92
Rannoch Strathtay Ballintium Bridge of Cally Airlie Balgavies
Fortingall A827 Balnaguard Blairgowrie Alyth Forfar Leysmill
Fearnan Aberfeldy Butterstone Blairgowrie A926 A933 Arbroath
Kenmore Dunkeld Caputh Spittalfield Meigle
Acharn Amulree Birnam Coupar Angus A92 Carnoustie
Bankfoot Stanley Cargill A923 Broughty Ferry
A822 Rait DUNDEE Tay Tentsmuir Forest
St Fillans A85 Guildtown Newport on Tay Leuchars
Methven A84 A85 Newburgh Balmerino Kilmany St. Andrews
Comrie A85 Crieff Findo Forteviot A914 Logie Boarhills
Gask Bridge of Earn Collessie Cupar S.Dron A917 Cellardyke Crail
Aberuthven Dunning Ladybank Largoward Anstruther
Auchterarder Glenfarg A91 Auchtermuchty Colinsburgh Pittenweem
Callander Blackford Gateside Falkland Lundin Links Elie
A9 Glendevon Balgedie A911 Lower Largo
Doune Dunblane Dollar Cleish M90 910
Alva A91 A823 A92 Firth of Forth
Blair Drummond Blairlogie A907 Dunfermline A900
A811 Stirling M9 Aberdour North Berwick
Fintry Bothkennar Inverkeithing Whitekirk
North Queensferry Aberlady Dunbar
A803 Reddingmuirhead Linlithgow Atheistaneford Innerwick
Kilsyth A80 EDINBURGH Cockburnspath Coldingham
A73 A8 Bolton B6355 Grantshouse Eyemouth
M8 West Calder Balerno A720 Pathead Abbey St. Bathans Reston Burnmouth
A8 A71 A70 A702 Humbie Longformacus B6355 Ayton
M74 West Linton Mordington BERWICK UPON TWEED
Law A72 Dunsyre Easter Deans Westruther Swinton
Lanark A701 A703 A697 Leitholm A698
Carmichael A73 Eddleston Birgham Coldstream
A72 Peebles Ednam B6352
Broughton Manor Kirkton Manor Galashiels Kelso Yetholm
A709 Melrose Bowden B6401 Morebattle
Yarrow Selkirk A68 A697
Ettrick Bridge Ashkirk Jedburgh A1
Elvanfoot A74 B1009 Minto A698
Denholm Camptown A68
Moffat B709 Hawick B6399
Teviothead A68
Thornhill A76 A7
B723 Boreland A7
Dunscore A701 A74 B6357 Newcastleton A68 A696
Dalry A702 Duncow Lochmaben Lockerbie
New Galloway Dumfries Canonbie A69 NEWCASTLE
Springholm Collin A69
Haugh of Urr Crocketford New Abbey Annan Gretna A68
A713 Beeswing Glencaple East Riggs
Castle Douglas A710 Kirkbean CARLISLE A66
Gatehouse of Fleet Palnackie Mainsriddle Southerness
Twynholm Kippford M6
Auchencairn Colvend Sandyhills A596
Borgue Kirkcudbright Rockcliffe A595 A66
Dundrennan ENGLAND
Solway Firth A66 A1(M)
A595 A5086 A66

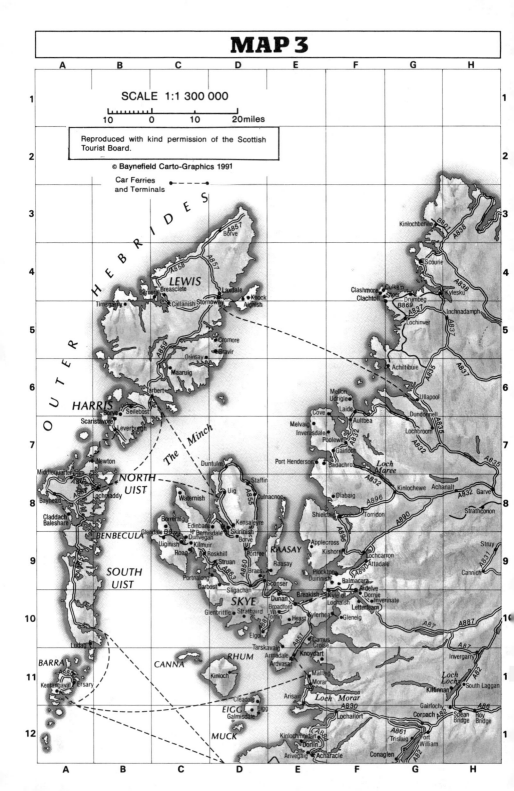

MAP 4

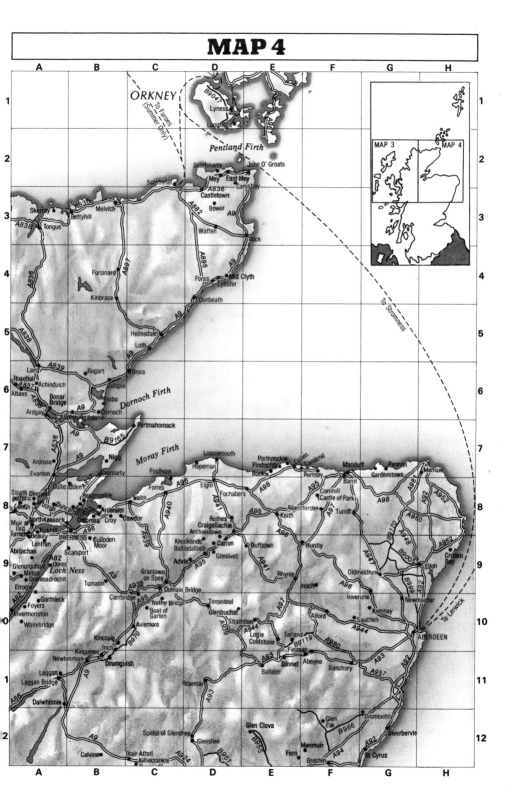

MAP 5

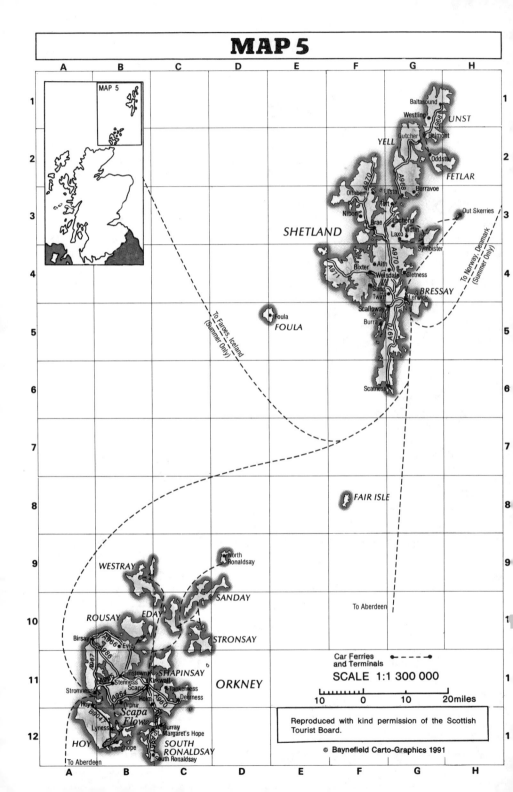

SCOTLAND HOME OF GOLF
A PASTIME PUBLICATION

I/We have seen your advertisement and wish to know if you have the following vacancy:

Name ....

Address ....

....

Dates from pm ....
Please give date and day of week in each case.

To am ....

Number in Party ....

Details of Children ....

(Please remember to include a stamped and addressed envelope with your enquiry)

SCOTLAND HOME OF GOLF
A PASTIME PUBLICATION

I/We have seen your advertisement and wish to know if you have the following vacancy:

Name ....

Address ....

....

Dates from pm ....
Please give date and day of week in each case.

To am ....

Number in Party ....

Details of Children ....

(Please remember to include a stamped and addressed envelope with your enquiry)

PASTIME GUIDES FOR 1994

Pastime Publications Ltd is one of the leading Holiday Guide Publishers for U.K. Bed & Breakfast, Self Catering and Farm & Country Holidays as well as Activity and Motoring Holidays in Scotland.

The following publications are useful guides and make wonderful gifts throughout the year.

Whilst our guides are available in leading bookshops and Tourist Board Centres for your convenience we will be happy to post a copy to you or send books as a gift for you. We will post overseas but have to charge separately for post or freight.

The inclusive cost of posting and packing your selection of guides to you and your friends in the U.K. is as follows:

☐ **Farm & Country Holidays**
This guide gives details of over 300 farms, many of them working with livestock, as well as activity holidays. **£4.20**

☐ **Bed & Breakfast Holidays**
A comprehensive guide to over 300 hotels, guesthouses, farms and inns throughout Britain. **£4.20**

☐ **Self Catering Holidays**
Includes details of hundreds of houses, chalets, boats, caravans, cottages, farms and flats throughout Britain. **£4.20**

☐ **Scotland for Fishing**
Permits, fishing rights, boat hire, season/dates, rods, fly fishing and spinning....it's all here. **£4.20**

☐ **Scotland Home of Golf**
Over 400 golf clubs featured. Also places to stay. Editorial by well-known celebrities. **£4.20**

☐ **Scotland for the Motorist**
Over 1,000 places of interest plus road maps and where to stay. **£4.20**

☐ **Scotland Activity Holidays**
The finest walks and trails as well as hill walking, cycling, skiing, yachting, canoeing and trekking.
£4.20

Tick your choice and send your order and payment to:
Pastime Publications Ltd., 32/34 Heriot Hill Terrace, Edinburgh EH7 4DY.
Telephone: 031-557 8092.
Deduct 10% for 2 or 3 titles and 20% for 4 or more titles.

Send to: NAME ....

ADDRESS ....

....POST CODE ....

I enclose Cheque/Postal Order for £..

SIGNATURE .... DATE ....

SCOTLAND HOME OF GOLF
A PASTIME PUBLICATION

I/We have seen your advertisement and wish to know if you have the following vacancy:

Name ....

Address ....

....

Dates from pm ....
Please give date and day of week in each case.
To am ....

Number in Party ....

Details of Children ....

(Please remember to include a stamped and addressed envelope with your enquiry)

SCOTLAND HOME OF GOLF
A PASTIME PUBLICATION

I/We have seen your advertisement and wish to know if you have the following vacancy:

Name ....

Address ....

....

Dates from pm ....
Please give date and day of week in each case.
To am ....

Number in Party ....

Details of Children ....

(Please remember to include a stamped and addressed envelope with your enquiry)

Notes

SCOTLAND HOME OF GOLF
A PASTIME PUBLICATION

I/We have seen your advertisement and wish to know if you have the following vacancy:

Name ....

Address ....

....

Dates from pm ....

Please give date and day of week in each case.

To am ....

Number in Party ....

Details of Children ....

*(Please remember to include a stamped and addressed envelope
with your enquiry)*

SCOTLAND HOME OF GOLF
A PASTIME PUBLICATION

I/We have seen your advertisement and wish to know if you have the following vacancy:

Name ....

Address ....

....

Dates from pm ....

Please give date and day of week in each case.

To am ....

Number in Party ....

Details of Children ....

*(Please remember to include a stamped and addressed envelope
with your enquiry)*

PASTIME GUIDES FOR 1994

Pastime Publications Ltd is one of the leading Holiday Guide Publishers for U.K. Bed & Breakfast, Self Catering and Farm & Country Holidays as well as Activity and Motoring Holidays in Scotland.

The following publications are useful guides and make wonderful gifts throughout the year.

Whilst our guides are available in leading bookshops and Tourist Board Centres for your convenience we will be happy to post a copy to you or send books as a gift for you. We will post overseas but have to charge separately for post or freight.

The inclusive cost of posting and packing your selection of guides to you and your friends in the U.K. is as follows:

☐ **Farm & Country Holidays**
This guide gives details of over 300 farms, many of them working with livestock, as well as activity holidays. **£4.20**

☐ **Scotland for Fishing**
Permits, fishing rights, boat hire, season/dates, rods, fly fishing and spinning....it's all here. **£4.20**

☐ **Bed & Breakfast Holidays**
A comprehensive guide to over 300 hotels, guesthouses, farms and inns throughout Britain. **£4.20**

☐ **Scotland Home of Golf**
Over 400 golf clubs featured. Also places to stay. Editorial by well-known celebrities. **£4.20**

☐ **Self Catering Holidays**
Includes details of hundreds of houses, chalets, boats, caravans, cottages, farms and flats throughout Britain. **£4.20**

☐ **Scotland for the Motorist**
Over 1,000 places of interest plus road maps and where to stay. **£4.20**

☐ **Scotland Activity Holidays**
The finest walks and trails as well as hill walking, cycling, skiing, yachting, canoeing and trekking.
£4.20

Tick your choice and send your order and payment to:
Pastime Publications Ltd., 32/34 Heriot Hill Terrace, Edinburgh EH7 4DY.
Telephone: 031-557 8092.
Deduct 10% for 2 or 3 titles and 20% for 4 or more titles.

Send to: NAME ....

ADDRESS ....

....POST CODE ....

I enclose Cheque/Postal Order for £ ....

SIGNATURE .... DATE ....